SPIRITS,
GHOSTS,
& DYBBUKS

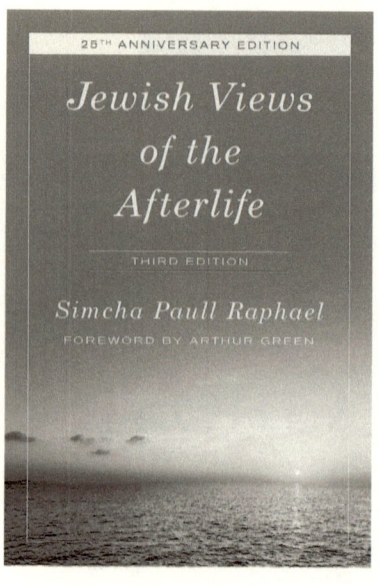

Originally published in 1994, *Jewish Views of the Afterlife* is a classic study of ideas of afterlife and postmortem survival in Jewish tradition and mysticism. As both a scholar and pastoral counselor, Raphael guides the reader through an exploration of over three millennia of Judaism's notions of afterlife and the fate of the individual after death. In addition, this book explores the implications of Jewish afterlife beliefs for a renewed understanding of traditional rituals, including funeral, burial, shiva, kaddish, and more. The twenty-fifth anniversary edition, published by Rowman & Littlefield in 2019, presents new material on little-known Jewish mystical teachings on reincarnation and a foreword by the renowned scholar of Jewish mysticism Rabbi Arthur Green. Both historical and contemporary, this book makes an important Jewish contribution to the growing contemporary psychology of death and dying and provides a rich resource for scholars, laypeople, teachers, and students.

JEWISH LIFE, DEATH, AND, TRANSITION SERIES

The Grief Journey and the Afterlife:
Jewish Pastoral Care for Bereavement

Living and Dying in Ancient Times:
Death, Burial, and Mourning in Biblical Tradition

May the Angels Carry You:
Jewish Prayers and Meditations for the Deathbed

Echoes from the Ashes:
Holocaust Poems of Life, Death and Re-Birth

Psalms in the Key of Healing:
A Text Study for Clergy, Chaplains and People Living with Illness

Jewish End-of-Life Care in a Virtual Age:
Our Traditions Reimagined

Musings with the Angel of Death:
Poems of Love, Life, and Longing

PRAISE FOR
SPIRITS, GHOSTS, & DYBBUKS:
AFTERLIFE JOURNEYS IN YIDDISH LORE

"Spirits, Ghosts, and Dybbuks: Afterlife Journeys in Yiddish Lore is a compelling and richly layered exploration of afterlife imagination in Yiddish-speaking Jewish culture. Simcha Paull Raphael masterfully weaves together folkloric, literary, and religious traditions to reveal how spirits and dybbuks were not merely feared or revered but served as powerful vessels of memory, communal anxiety, and personal longing.

This book is a significant and timely contribution to the study of Jewish afterlife narratives, offering ethical depth and cultural resonance. *Spirits, Ghosts, and Dybbuks: Afterlife Journeys in Yiddish Lore* is as intellectually illuminating as it is evocative—an essential work for scholars and readers interested in how the stories of the dead continue to shape the lives of the living."

> Dr. Nicole Bauer, Assistant Professor
> of Religious Studies, University of Graz,
> Co-editor of *Ideas of Possession:*
> *Interdisciplinary and Transcultural Perspectives*

"This book is a fascinating exploration of the paradox that just as religious thinkers influenced by modernity were rejecting all ideas about an afterlife, Yiddish writers such as Sholem Aleichem, I.L. Peretz, Isaac Bashevis Singer, and others, were exploring these beliefs and incorporating them into their stories and novels. Simcha Paull Raphael has brought together material from all these writers in a

book that will enlighten its readers and inform them of a world gone by."

"Simcha Paull Raphael is the master guide into the terrain of Jewish views of the afterlife, offering clarity, context, and attention to detail. In this presentation of Yiddish tales of the other side of the grave, we are entertained, expanded by possibilities, and inherently invited to discern our own beliefs."

"*Spirits, Ghosts, and Dybbuks: Afterlife Journeys in Yiddish Lore* provides an intriguing and accessible look into beliefs about the afterlife in Yiddish folk and popular culture from the 16th through the 20th centuries. In his past works, Simcha Paull Raphael has introduced readers to the deep teachings about death and the afterlife found in classical Jewish sources. In this book, he turns to folk literature and the evidence of modern writers in Yiddish to show how spirits of those who are no longer in this world communicate their presence to the living, and were a daily presence to ordinary Jews."

"The old shall be renewed,
and the new shall be made holy."

— Rabbi Avraham Yitzhak Kook

Published in conjunction with the DA'AT INSTITUTE for Death Awareness, Advocacy and Training

Chapters 2-7 of this title, with some changes made for the present volume, were originally published as Chapter Ten, "Spirits, Ghosts and Dybbuks in Yiddish Literature," in the 3rd edition of *Jewish Views of the Afterlife* by Simcha Paull Raphael (Rowman & Littlefield, 2019). All rights reserved. The author and publisher thank Rowman & Littlefield for their generous permission to republish this material here.

Albion-Andalus Books
P. O. Box 19852
Boulder, CO 80308
albionandalus.com

Design & composition by Albion-Andalus Books

Cover design by Scott Fray

Front cover image created by Scott Fray with the assistance of Midjourney, an AI image-generation tool, based on a scene from the Yiddish film *Der Dibuk* (1937) directed by Michał Waszyński.

ISBN-13: 978-1-953220-48-6

SPIRITS,
GHOSTS,
& DYBBUKS

AFTERLIFE JOURNEYS
IN YIDDISH LORE

SIMCHA PAULL RAPHAEL

Albion
Andalus
Boulder, Colorado
2025

*Dedicated to my grandparents
who left the Old World of Yiddish culture
and built lives for themselves
and their families in the New World*

Myron Palefsky (1893-1969)
Jenny Mendelson Palefsky (1896-1981)

Theodor Geiger (1890-1933)
Mina Kornfeld Geiger (1897-1955)

Contents

FOREWORD

Not long ago I visited Lincoln Park Cemetery, in Warwick, Rhode Island, to have a conversation with my mother, may she rest in peace. We had a few things to talk about, so I stood at her grave and spoke with her. The conversation was easier now that she is in the World of Truth. Some time later, as the mysteries of fate would have it, I was invited to write a Foreword for the book that you now hold in your hands.

The subject of spirits, ghosts, and dybbuks is a worthy one, but why focus specifically on Yiddish? After all, there is an abundant Jewish literature on these subjects in Hebrew and Aramaic, much of which is quoted and referenced in the following pages. Menasseh ben Israel's book, *Nishmat Ḥayyim* (Amsterdam, 1651), is by itself a trove of such accounts. And similar material can be found in other cultures and languages. In the abstract, sticking to Yiddish might seem like an arbitrary choice: would Isaac Bashevis Singer's stories have been any less worthy of inclusion if he had written them in English?

A first answer: The choice is not so much about the Yiddish language, but about *Yidishkayt*, the culture-world of those whose means of expression was, and is, the Yiddish language.

A second answer: There is something special about the place of the Yiddish language in this culture. *Yidishkayt* is, one might say, a tale told in *two* languages, Hebrew—called *loshn koydesh*, the holy tongue—and Yiddish, called *mame-loshn*, one's mother-tongue. Yiddish is essentially a secular language. Some pious Jews today, even in Israel, believe that Hebrew is too holy for secular use; for that purpose, they speak Yiddish. Yet, paradoxically, Yiddish is a secular language permeated by religiosity. Just one homely example will suffice. In Yiddish, toilet paper is *asher-yotser-papir*, named for the blessing that observant Jews recite after going to the bathroom, giving thanks for the miracle of a body that can separate nutrients from waste matter. An atheist seeking to buy this humble item from a Yiddish-speaking vendor can't avoid referencing these words of prayer.

Yiddish is thus itself between two worlds. Jewish religion, including its spirits, dybbuks, and exorcisms, haunts Yiddish the same way spirits and dybbuks haunt the world of Yiddish-speakers. A case can be made that it is the perfect medium for telling tales of events that take place between the two worlds of the living and the dead. Except perhaps the author of the *Ma'aseh Book*, the other writers discussed here were unavoidably tinged by modernity, and yet as Yiddish speakers had a foot in both the modern world and the world of tradition. This unique perspective shines through many of the works discussed here.

Spirits, Ghosts, and Dybbuks: Afterlife Journeys in Yiddish Lore is not a mere academic study, though it is that as well. As Simcha Paull Raphael concludes—speaking in his own voice—that "between the world of the living and the world of the dead is a window not a wall." Or, perhaps, we should say *many* windows. The windows through which our ancestors looked and spoke with *their* ancestors have, for many of us, been bricked over by modernity and scientific materialism. We can see in the different colored brickwork where they used to be—Raphael points out many of them—but we may not be able to uncover them. Max Weber spoke of the "disenchantment of the world," a phenomenon that affects many of us. The world of ghosts and spirit possession has lost much of its plausibility. Can we transcend this disenchantment? Raphael drops a hint near the very end: we can feel connected in "synchronistic moments" with our loved ones whose physical existence has ended. Jewish teaching is clear about this synchrony. Time is not like an arrow (as modern thought would have it), but more like a unidirectional spiral staircase. As we climb, we come round to places where we, and others, have been before, and we can look down and connect with them. We don't merely recall the past: we can re-experience it. We were all present at the Exodus; we all stood at Sinai. Reb Shmelke of Nikolsburg, the great Hasidic *rebbe*, once recited the Song of the Sea with such fervor that those present raised the hems of their garments, for fear that they would get wet as they walked through the Red Sea. More humbly, how many of us feel quite palpably the presence at the Passover Seder of family members who are no longer there physically?

We may not conceptualize these moments of connection in terms of spirits or dybbuks, but they are as real and profound as anything we could wish for. And in this book you will find a treasure-house of wisdom exploring these mystifying topics. Thank you Simcha Paull Raphael for inviting us into these hidden worlds.

Rabbi Jacob Adler, Ph.D.
Department of Philosophy,
University of Arkansas,
Fayetteville, AK

PREFACE

My mother was Canadian-born, although her parents were both native Yiddish-speakers, immigrants from Roumania, or what was then the Austro-Hungarian Empire. Growing up in the 1950s and '60s, there were two folk traditions my mother repeatedly practiced, and bequeathed to me: 1) If someone could not find an object in our home, my mother would say: "Turn over a glass and put it in the window;" and 2) Whenever we finished doing homework, or reading a book, she always told me and my two brothers: "Don't leave an opened page, close the book!" There was never any explanation, other than that she learned these from her mother.

As an adult, in my studies of Jewish history and tradition, I learned about Aramaic incantation bowls—inscribed pottery dating from the fifth to the seventh centuries C.E. in Babylonia and the Fertile Crescent.[1] Written in Aramaic, these bowls had a theurgic, magical quality to them, and were often found strategically placed upside down in the four corners of a home. For what purpose? As the inscribed incantations revealed, they were there to trap demonic agents! Unbeknownst to my mother, she had learned from her mother, and likely back through generations, a practice of turning over a glass, seemingly a substitute for an Aramaic incantation bowl, to trap those demons hiding lost items for which we had been searching. And not leaving books open? One respects a sacred text by closing the pages of the book.

But more: folk tradition taught that if one left open a sacred text, there were angelic presences that would cause one to forget their learning (Yoreh Deah 277).

My mother had no idea of any mystical or folk roots of these practices. But she did a have a mother born into the Yiddish cultural life of Eastern European Jewry, replete with wonder-working Hasidic Rabbis and invisible worlds populated by otherworldly beings, mischievous demons, and souls of deceased teachers and relatives.

With the migration from Eastern Europe to the shores of North America, the mythos of that world of multidimensional beings slowly disappeared. Impacted by rationalistic modernity, and then the trauma of the Holocaust, the cultural environment of Jews and Judaism that once believed in realms of angelic guides, visitors from the world beyond, afterlife, and the survival of consciousness after death essentially vanished in the mid-twentieth century.

In this book, I aspire to bring to light lost Eastern European Jewish traditions of spirits, ghosts, and dybbuks—disembodied wandering and confused spirits that attach themselves to living people and animals. This book is a continuation of the work I have done, resurrecting the mythic worldview of my grandmother by writing on Jewish views of the afterlife for the past four decades. The afterlife stories of Yiddish folk culture are so fascinating, and I am delighted to be able to share this material through this book.

In the aftermath of the Covid epidemic, the nature of our work life has radically changed for many people. The "work from home" lifestyle means spending hours and days in front of a computer or tablet. I know this personally as a psychotherapist, where over 80% of my client work is online. Coupled with being a scholar committed to research and writing, life can be isolating.

My antidote to this, besides robust Shabbat and Yom Tov dinners in my home with friends and family, is to have a small posse of close friends with whom I share—both in person and through regular Zoom and telephone conversations—the ups, downs, and challenges of life in our times. I offer my thanks for being on the journey with me in love and friendship to the following people: Rabbi Avruhm Addison, Erich DeHaven, Rabbi Nadya Gross, Cole Imperi, Lynn Ireland, Elliott Isenberg, Rabbi Myriam Klotz, Rabbi David Levin, Herb Levine, Rabbi Andrea Lobel, Rabbi Steven Nathan, Rabbi Rochelle Robins, Rabbi Jacob Staub, Stephen Stober, Jim Tornetta, and Rabbi Ziona Zelazo. I couldn't do this without you. And to my spiritual guides and healers, Michele Saffier and Rabbi Lavey Derby, thanks for having my back.

I am ever-grateful for my family. To my two children, Yigdal and Hallel: Thank you for tolerating your eccentric parents and bringing deep fulfillment to my life. And to my creative and multi-talented wife, Rabbi Geela Rayzel Raphael: You have been a beloved friend, co-parenting partner, and spiritual companion on our shared life journey for more than half my life. At this stage in the family life process, we are watching our adult children fashion meaningful lives for themselves in work and love. And we are blessed with aging gracefully in the eighth decade of our lives. Thanks for the love, laughter, and creative and business ventures we share, and thanks for making Shabbos with me since we first met in 1984. I feel blessed by your consistent support as I do the writing I love. I look forward to many more years (and books) together.

This is the eighth book in the *Jewish Life, Death and Transition* series, published by Albion-Andalus Books, in collaboration with the DA'AT Institute for Death Awareness, Advocacy and Training. I thank Netanel Miles-Yépez of Albion-Andalus Books for his vision to create this series, and Daniel Jami for his thoughtful and gentle editorial wisdom midwifing this book to publication. I thank Noelle Lee of Bloomsbury Publishing for making it possible to use material from *Jewish Views of the Afterlife* in this book, and I acknowledge and thank my friend and colleague, Rabbi Jacob Adler, for his thoughtful Foreword to this book. And finally, my heartfelt thanks to my friend Scott Fray for his awesome artistic acumen and creativity in designing the cover for this book.

At this juncture of my life journey, I am filled with gratitude for the opportunity to share the fruits of my creativity with others. In devotion, I acknowledge the Source of Life, the Holy One of Blessing who has given us life and vitality, sustained us, and brought us to this moment.

Simcha Paull Raphael
Melrose Park, PA
July 1st, 2025 (My 74th birthday)

1

A PERSONAL JOURNEY

In Search of Jewish Views of the Afterlife

In 1973 my closest friend Leslie Erdos was killed in a traffic accident. He was alive and well one Saturday afternoon, we were laughing and enjoying each other's company as we had done for many years since we first met in high school. We both had plans for the evening, so we said our goodbyes around dinner time. At 5:00 AM that night, in the middle of a deep sleep, I heard the phone ring. I still remember it as if it were yesterday. The voice on the other end of the phone, a mutual friend, was blunt and direct: "Steve [my name at the time], Leslie's dead!" Those three words changed the course of my life forever.

By the next morning, plans were being made for Leslie's burial, to be held at Mt. Pleasant Memorial Park, in a Montreal suburb. I promise you there was absolutely nothing pleasant about burying a twenty-three-year-old young man in the dead of winter. But the amazing thing was, very early on, I felt a sense of his presence. Shivering in the ice-cold weather at the cemetery, it was as if I could feel him standing next to me watching over the burial ritual, and other friends present shared having had a similar experience. During the week of shivah, on at least one occasion, a few friends remarked that we felt Leslie's presence in the room. Then, a few months later, my friend appeared to me very vividly in a dream, and it was not an ordinary dream; I experienced it as if he were visiting from wherever he was in the realm of the dead.

While in shock for months after this traumatic death, the subjective perceptions of an afterlife communication I had experienced activated a deep desire to know what Judaism had to say about life after death. Growing up, my family were members of a modern Orthodox synagogue, and in university, while completing an Honours degree in History and Philosophy of Religion, I had studied the Bible, Jewish history and thought, Eastern religions, and more—but no one had ever taught or talked about the afterlife in Judaism. Yet from studies of world religions, I knew teachings on the survival of the soul after death were found in traditions all across the planet. My inquis- itiveness to discover what Judaism had to say about the afterlife was repeatedly met with a glaring dearth of information. First of all, at that time, very few books had been published in English on death and Judaism. Those studies, by and large, delineated legalistic-halakhic prac- tices of Jewish death rituals, with almost no philosophical speculation on what happens after death. Secondly, what- ever I did read on afterlife in Judaism conveyed the message that Jews don't believe in life after death. Judaism celebrates life and the living, the here and now, and does not dwell upon the hereafter was the normative credo I encountered.[2] There were references to ideas about the resurrection of the dead at the end of historical time, but I could not find Jewish teachings about the fate of the individual immediately after death. There was nothing in Judaism that helped to explain the experiences I was having of my friend's presence intermittently peering through the veil between life and death, between this world and the world beyond.

This was my dilemma as a grief-stricken, spiritually curious young man.

Meeting Reb Zalman

A few years later, I was fortunate to meet the man who would become my teacher and mentor, Rabbi Zalman Schachter-Shalomi, of blessed memory, a renowned teacher of Jewish mysticism and spirituality and founder of the contemporary Jewish Renewal movement. In our first conversation, I remember speaking with Reb Zalman (as he was affectionately known) about Tibetan Buddhism and Kabbalah, interests of mine at the time. He piqued my curiosity by mentioning two texts that were, as he put it, "equivalents of the Tibetan Book of the Dead." Though I was not aware of it when we first met, I later discovered that Reb Zalman himself had studied psychic phenomena, parapsychology, spiritualism, and near-death experiences, as well as the writings of the Swedish mystic Emanuel Swedenborg and the British Society for Psychical Research. In his own questioning of "what happens after we die?" Reb Zalman found in these various sources parallels to teachings in Kabbalah.[3] I was relieved to know there were Jewish teachings on life after death, though I still needed both a map and a tour guide. Unbeknownst to me at that time, a seed was planted in that encounter for future explorations of this elusive topic of the afterlife in Judaism, and Reb Zalman would be the one to provide a map to explore and serve as the tour guide.

In 1977, I began a doctoral program at the California Institute of Integral Studies[4] in San Francisco, exploring spiritually-based approaches to counseling and psychotherapy. Less than two years into my studies, in early 1979, I met up with Reb Zalman once again on one of his teaching trips to the San Francisco Bay area. Updating him on work I had been doing for my Ph.D., he inquired: "What will you do for your doctoral dissertation?" He was, after all, an academic who held positions at different universities throughout his life. I told him I had written papers on death and the afterlife in Eastern thought. Although I was uncertain about what came next, I mentioned that I was considering writing on some aspect of death and Judaism. "Good!" he replied. "Here is what you will do. Read these books," he said, writing down the names of the two traditional Jewish texts on life after death he had mentioned in Montreal years earlier. "You will write your dissertation on death and the afterlife in Judaism. I will be on your committee." Flabbergasted, I did not know what to say. I certainly felt a resonant moment of truth. Reb Zalman was known to be able to call people into their life destiny, and in that moment, he certainly did that for me.

After completing my doctoral coursework, I spent the next five years reading everything I could get my hands on about death and the afterlife in Judaism and world religions. In good academic fashion, I titled my doctoral dissertation, *Judaism's Contribution to the Psychology of Death and Dying.*[5] Reb Zalman, Dr. David Bakan, author of *Sigmund Freud and the Jewish Mystical Tradition*, and Dr.

Ralph Metzner, a pioneering researcher in psychedelics, and Dean of the California Institute of Integral Studies, served as my dissertation committee. Only in California in the 1970s and '80s could one write a Psychology dissertation on life after death in Judaism (and Tibetan Buddhism and Theosophy) with practical applications for working with the dying and bereaved. It was certainly an exciting adventure doing the "spiritual archeology" of recovering little-known Jewish teachings on the afterlife, and simultaneously envisioning new pathways in the psychology of compassionate care for people on the end-of-life journey and those dealing with grief and loss.

From Philosophy to Praxis to Publication

After receiving my doctorate in June of 1986, my first job was as a resident psychologist at Benjamin's Park Memorial Chapel, a Jewish funeral home, in Toronto, Canada. I was hired to develop a community death awareness program and bereavement support services in a city of 150,000 Jews. While I had read voraciously about death and the afterlife for years, all of a sudden, I was called to be present with families dealing with suicide, murder, infant death, and a variety of both commonplace and traumatic deaths. In providing education, offering counseling, and leading bereavement groups, I frequently had opportunities to apply philosophy to practice and find ways of comforting the bereaved, from a spiritual point of view that assumed the continuity of consciousness after death. Experiences I had working at the funeral home inspired and guided my work as a death awareness educator and grief counselor for the decades which followed, and until this day.

Around the same time, I signed a contract to expand and rework my doctoral dissertation into a book, and in 1994, the resulting *Jewish Views of the Afterlife* was published by Jason Aronson. My primary goal in that book was to demonstrate that the notion that Judaism does not have a belief in afterlife survival of the soul was a misconception of modernity, not the whole picture. Do *Jews* believe in an afterlife? Well, some do, and some don't. From the time of modernity onwards, secular beliefs have always been an acceptable part of Jewish intellectual life.[6] But does *Judaism* believe in an afterlife? In the pre-modern Jewish world, there were never existential questions about life after death; traditional Jews of the shtetl did not sit around having philosophical discourse about whether there was an afterlife. Notions of survival after death were hardwired into the Jewish understanding of what it means to be a human being.

Jewish Views of the Afterlife synthesized material from the Bible, Apocrypha, rabbinic tradition, medieval philosophy and midrash, Kabbalah, and Hasidism to delineate the extensive historical dimensions of Judaism's teaching on life after death and postmortem survival. In a sense, I wrote the book I would have wanted to read as a young man traumatized by the sudden death of my friend.

A second edition of *Jewish Views of the Afterlife* was published by Rowman and Littlefield fifteen years later, in 2009. Drawing from my teaching and bereavement counseling, as well as rabbinic experience facilitating death rituals for the dying and bereaved, I authored new material on "Afterlife and the Renewal of Jewish Death

Rituals." Having previously documented the array of Jewish afterlife teachings throughout history, I asked the question: "If we start with the assumption that consciousness survives bodily death, how does that transform ways we think about Jewish rituals of deathbed *vidui*, funeral, burial, shivah, Kaddish, Yizkor and Yahrzeit?" This fundamental question has characterized my work for the past twenty-five years, or more, and I have frequently taught about how Jewish death rituals have a "soul-guiding" dimension that help to facilitate the postmortem journey for the deceased.[7]

In 2019, Rowman and Littlefield published a 25th anniversary, third edition of *Jewish Views of the Afterlife*, in which I authored an entirely new chapter on "Spirits, Ghosts, and Dybbuks in Yiddish Literature," and this book is based upon an expansion of that chapter, with permission from Rowman & Littlefield.

Goal of This Book

When I originally wrote *Jewish Views of the Afterlife*, I maintained that in the mid-nineteenth century, with modernity and the proliferation of rationalism and scientific materialism, ideas of the afterlife vanished from public, communal concern in the Jewish world. The early proponents of the Haskalah, the Jewish enlightenment, redefined Judaism as a religion of reason and weeded out non-rational, mystical elements, including belief in the survival of the soul after death. However, over the years, ongoing exploration of postmortem themes and motifs in Judaism revealed that beliefs in the afterlife, although ignored by twentieth-century scholars and philosophers of Jewish thought, were showing up in short stories, novels, and plays of Eastern European Yiddish authors. In literary fantasy and folk culture, traditional Jewish motifs of postmortem survival were being ingeniously interwoven with social and political commentaries on Eastern European Jewish life. Despite modernity, secularism, and scientific rationalism, Jewish ideas of life after death persisted, albeit in a wide swath of secular Yiddish fiction.

The task of this book is to demonstrate how themes of traditional Jewish eschatology and motifs of afterlife survival made their way into the literary creations of late medieval and early modern Yiddish literature. The chapters that follow are filled with depictions of spirits, wandering ghosts, and dybbuks—malevolent discarnate beings that possess the body of a living person—plus literary allusions to ideas of Gehenna, the underworld realm of purgation, and the heavenly Garden of Eden, as well as conversations about the Jewish doctrine of *gilgul* (reincarnation).

While the religious texts of biblical, rabbinic, medieval, and kabbalistic tradition were written in either Hebrew or Aramaic, and considered *sifrei kodesh*—holy writings, i.e. religious texts per se—in this book we explore a definitively secular genre of literature, written in Yiddish in Central and Eastern Europe between the sixteenth and twentieth centuries, and in some cases, in twentieth century America.

The genre of Yiddish literature is a unique goldmine for uncovering images and themes of postmortem survival of the dead. The narratives we explore in the chapters that follow demonstrate unequivocally how, despite scientific materialism and Haskalah rationalism, attachment to age-old Jewish ideas of the afterlife persisted throughout the modern era, and into contemporary times. In the final analysis, this book documents a literary testament to the enduring persistence of the Jewish belief in the survival of human consciousness after death.

Today there is a growing contemporary interest in life after death, and a wide proliferation of writings on near-death experiences, survival after death, and the afterlife beliefs and rituals of Indigenous, Celtic, Eastern, and other traditions. Additionally, there are both fictional and documentary-style programs on spirit mediums who speak with the dead, and numerous movies and television series that portray characters communicating with the deceased, as well as returning with memories of past lives. Despite the omnipresence of a secular, scientific cultural-worldview, there is clearly an intense interest in the topic of life after death. In highlighting afterlife themes in Yiddish literature, this book makes a small, but focused, contribution to that growing body of writings, video, and film on the postmortem survival of the soul.

2

YIDDISH:
THE LANGUAGE AND LITERATURE
OF EASTERN EUROPEAN JEWISH LIFE

The Creation and Evolution of Yiddish Literature

To begin our journey entering into Eastern European Jewish lore, it is necessary to first present a brief overview of the development of Yiddish language and literature. Yiddish emerged as the vernacular of Ashkenazic Jewry in the Rhine Valley, in the early eleventh century. A fusion language synthesizing Middle High German, with Hebrew and Aramaic, and a small smattering of proto-Romance language, it rapidly became the lingua franca of Jews in Central, Western, and Eastern Europe. While originally Yiddish was predominantly a lived, spoken oral tradition, over time, a unique character of Yiddish literature began to evolve. The earliest surviving literary document in Yiddish, dating back to 1272, is a rhymed blessing found in the *Mahzor Worms*, a festival prayerbook according to the Ashkenazi rite of the Jews in Worms, Germany.[8] Subsequent to the development of the printing press, in the fifteenth century, Yiddish literature began to proliferate and spread widely throughout Europe. To meet the needs of the masses of Jews who had a minimal and imperfect knowledge of Hebrew, publishing houses in most major European cities began printing a diverse assortment of Yiddish books that included: translations of the Hebrew Bible; translations of Psalms; Biblical epics; homiletical prose, ethical literature—morality books (*musar*) and books of conduct (*minhagim*); prayer books for women; as well as Yiddish poetry; and once the modern era began, a splendid panoply of fiction—short stories and novels capturing the lived essence of daily life of the European Jews as they struggled with the impact of modernity and enlightenment on traditional culture.[9] Very rapidly these varied Yiddish writings became ubiquitous throughout the far-reaching geographical areas of urban and rural Jewish communities in Central, Western, and Eastern Europe.[10] And to take a leap across geography and history: with the mass exodus of Jews from Czarist Russia in the late nineteenth century, Yiddish literature in America captured and expressed the realities of life for the first generation of Eastern European Jews who had landed on the shores of the United States, the "*goldene medinah.*"[11]

Among the earliest Yiddish books were:

1. The *Bovo-Bukh* (1541), by Elia Levita, is a poetic collection of chivalric romance tales that spawned the creation of a secular Jewish literature. Exceptionally popular, this book was published in over forty editions over the course of four centuries.[12]

2. *Tsena-Urena* (1622), by Jacob ben Isaac Ashkenazi, a rendering in Yiddish of weekly portions of Torah and Haftorah, augmented with rabbinic lore and legend from midrash, Talmud and other commentators. Sometimes called "The Women's

Bible," this celebrated Yiddish work was specifically designed to make the heritage of rabbinic Torah teachings accessible to young women. For three centuries, the *Tsena-Urena* was regarded as the most treasured book in the Jewish home.

3. Also, a benchmark book of Yiddish literature, where we will soon begin our exploration of themes of afterlife survival, is the *Ma'aseh Book*, an early seventeenth-century collection of Yiddish stories interweaving both ancient rabbinic legend and contemporary folk narratives. An exceptionally popular book in its time, and reprinted in more than twenty editions over the course of two centuries,[13] the pages of the *Ma'aseh Book* are filled with supernatural tales of demons, witches, spirits, ghosts, and the earliest published dybbuk stories— tales of lost and confused spirits that possess living beings.[14]

Another important evolutionary step in the development of Yiddish literature was the work of Sholom Yankev Abramovitch (1836-1919), known by his literary persona—Mendele Mocher Sforim, Mendele the Bookseller—a character of his fictional writings. Considered the grandfather of Yiddish literature, with his first novel, *Dos kleyne mentshele* ("The Little Person") published in 1864, Abramovitch catalyzed the transformation of modern Yiddish into a literary language of great artistic potential and creativity. Although Yiddish had been the common speech of millions of Jews in Europe, before Mendele (as he was called), Yiddish literature was predominantly associated with women's books, somewhat scorned and not held in the same esteem as scholarly Hebrew writings.[15] However, in the closing decades of the nineteenth century Mendele and his contemporaries, in particular Sholem Aleichem and I.L. Peretz, generated a fertile efflorescence of Yiddish literature.[16] Printed pages of books, newspapers, and, journals were suffused with a creative mélange of short story and novel, poetry and prose, theater and political polemic. The whole genre of Yiddish literature was vitalized with a new spirit of creativity, and vernacular Yiddish of the old shtetl Jew transformed into a vibrant literary form.

And further: as the values of the Enlightenment and the Jewish Haskalah were embraced in Central and Eastern Europe, the longstanding relationship Jews had to Torah, Talmud, *halakha*, and, rabbinic leadership was radically challenged, eroded and, slowly but surely, transformed.[17] Abramovitch and his contemporaries wrestled daily and deeply with the complexities of modernity, secularization, rejection of traditional religion, progressive movements for social change, and the nascent Zionist movement advocating for a Jewish state. In their writings, they captured the nuances, conflicts and also the absurdity and humor of the clash between the old and new, between the life of the shtetl and radical changes being brought about by the emergent qualities of Jewish secular and political thinking of the times. Out of this dynamic and fertile quagmire of cultural transformation emerged a rich tapestry of creative literary vignettes documenting the widespread belief of Eastern European Jews in the survival of consciousness after death.

Sources of Afterlife Writings in Yiddish Literature

To uncover a variegated assortment of afterlife images in Yiddish literature, this book will explore the following sources:

1. The *Ma'aseh Book* (1602), a collection of Yiddish folk tales, which in particular has seven different stories of wandering ghosts, discarnate beings, and dybbuks that have interactive encounters and, in many cases, verbal conversations with living human beings;

2. Writings of Solomon Naumovich Rabinovich, better known by his pen name Sholem Aleichem (1859-1916), and in particular stories of *Tevye the Dairyman* (written between 1899-1909), which later became immortalized in film and theater versions of *Fiddler on the Roof*;

3. Writings of Isaac Leib Peretz (I.L. Peretz) (1852-1915), a prolific Polish-born writer, whose novels and short stories are imbued with a sense of mystical understanding of Kabbalah. Specifically, we shall explore two representative stories of his work: "What is the Soul?" (1890) and "Bontshe Shvayg" (1894);

4. The uniquely famous play *The Dybbuk or Between Two Worlds*, by Shloyme Zanvl Rappoport, known by his pseudonym S. An-sky (1863-1920), originally written in 1914, and first staged in Warsaw in 1920; and

5. Writings of the Nobel Laureate, Isaac Bashevis Singer, (1904-1991), who wrote in Yiddish both in Poland and America. We shall consider his earliest novel, *Satan in Goray* (1933); a famous short story, "Sabbath in Gehenna" (1972); and, to round out our historical exploration of Yiddish literature, *Shadows on the Hudson*, (1957) a modern-era novel about Holocaust survivors living in New York after World War II and wrestling with the meaning of life, death, and suffering.

In studying these various literary sources, we shall show how traditional Jewish afterlife teachings are interwoven within Yiddish literature, and also highlight the unique ways these multihued Yiddish writings about ghosts, spirits, and dybbuks were influenced by, and embodied the emerging intellectual and cultural worldview of modernity.

3

IMAGES OF AFTERLIFE
IN THE *MA'ASEH BOOK*

Background

Composed anonymously in the late sixteenth century, and published by Jacob ben Abraham, in Basel, Switzerland in 1602, the *Ma'aseh Book*—literally "Book of Stories"—was written in a simple style, specifically for both men and women lacking skills in Hebrew language and literature. An anthology of 257 stories, in vernacular Yiddish, this book is comprised of three parts: 1) 157 stories from Talmud and midrash, elaborated and embellished;[18] 2) a selection of 25 stories told of the spiritual leaders of Hasidei Ashkenaz—a medieval German mystical community from the tenth to fourteen centuries—Rabbi Yehuda he-Hasid (Judah the Pious), and his father Rabbi Samuel he-Hasid (Samuel the Pious);[19] and 3) a diverse collection of 75 narrative stories from both Jewish and non-Jewish sources, many of these recounting tales and legends of central European folk traditions.[20] Attesting to the popularity of this collection of stories, the *Ma'aseh Book* was reprinted in Yiddish at least twenty times, and has been translated into German, French and English.[21]

In the *Ma'aseh Book* are descriptions of how spirits of the deceased are in open communication with the world of the living. Night dreams, visions, apparitions, and even a hostile possession of another's body and mind are some of ways in which discarnate spirits make their presence known. As the tales of the *Ma'aseh Book* reveal, in the mindset of medieval Jewish folk culture, the invisible world was ever-alive with ghosts, ghoulish shades, dybbuks, and even wise beings who died and returned for friendly visitations.

The Dead Visit the Living

Retelling a Talmudic legend, the *Ma'aseh Book* relates a story of the second century CE Rabbi Yehuda Ha-Nasi returning to visit with family members after his death.[22]

> When Rabbi [Yehuda Ha-Nasi] was dying, he called his children to him and said to them: "My dear children, I am lying on my deathbed and desire to make my will. Take care of your mother. Keep a light always burning on my table. Let the table be always set and the bed neatly covered with white sheets, for I will come back every Friday night to my house and pronounce the *kiddush*." And he did return.
>
> One Friday evening, as he was sitting in his house, a neighbor came and knocked on the door, wishing to come in. The servant said: "No one is allowed to come in, for Rabbi is here." When

Rabbi [Yehuda Ha-Nasi] heard this, he
disappeared and never came on a Sabbath eve.[23]

Embedded in this story are a few different ideas
about life after death. First and foremost, the *Ma'aseh Book*
communicates not only that there is a consciousness after
death, but that beings from the other side can choose to
interact with the world of the living. Here, Rabbi Yehuda
visits his family on Shabbat, not as a frightening or confused ghostly figure, but in a very loving way. This notion
is certainly resonant with teachings of Kabbalah that sug-
gest the postmortem soul can remain in relationship with
the world of the living. The Zohar, a mystical commentary on the Torah from thirteen-century Spain, speaks of
how the spirit of the deceased "goes forth roaming the
world," particularly in the first year after death (Zohar
I, 226a-226b). Also significant here is that after a certain
point in time, Rabbi Yehuda no longer returns home for
a friendly Shabbat visit. This concept is also borne out
in kabbalistic texts, which teach that after twelve months
the soul leaves behind terrestrial attachments and dons a
celestial garment, as it prepares to enter Gan Eden (the
heavenly Garden of Eden) (Zohar II, 210b). However, it
is interesting to note that Rabbi Yehuda ceases his family
visitations when he is accidentally "outed" to a neighbor
by his servant. This reveals that, even if the culture did
have an awareness that deceased beings can interact with
the living, just as today, people can be very uncomfortable
about spirits of the dead coming around to visit. Rabbi
Yehuda decided it was time for his sojourns into the world
of the living to end.

The Dead Provide Information to the Living

In another legend redacted from Talmudic tradition,[24] R. Ze'iri goes to the grave of a deceased woman and inquires as to the whereabouts of his saddlebag that had been in her possession. She offers him the specific information he needs to be able to track the location of his lost object. The story communicates the idea that spirits of the dead are aware of the goings on in the world of the living:

> R' Ze'iri left a saddle-bag in the care of a woman to keep until he returned from the house of his teacher. When he returned from his teacher, he found that the woman had died. So he went to the cemetery to the grave of the woman and asked her what had become of the saddle-bag which he had left in her care. And she replied: "You ask me concerning the saddle-bag you left in my charge until you returned from your teacher. I have taken good care of it. Therefore, go back to the house and you will find it in the hole where the bolt of the door enters." He went to the house to look for it and found it exactly in the spot where the woman had told him.[25]

What is interesting in this story is that communication between the living and the dead takes place at a cemetery. In medieval times it was not uncommon to go the grave of a loved one, or a famous teacher, and make petitionary requests to the deceased. In his comprehensive study, *Jewish Magic and Superstition—A Study in Folk Religion*, Joshua Trachtenberg lists a number of petitionary invocations to the deceased performed at the grave, some of which were condemned, others tolerated by authorities.[26] In the kabbalistic community of Safed in the sixteenth and seventeenth centuries, Isaac Luria, Chaim Vital and their colleagues and students frequently practiced grave-side visitation for the sake of inquiring of the spirits of the dead.[27] This practice of gravesite communing with deceased spirits was not uncommon in the world in which the *Ma'aseh Book* was published. Even to this day, there remains a vibrant tradition of petitioning spiritual inter-cession at the gravesites of the late Lubavitcher Rebbe,[28] Rabbi Nahman of Bratslav, Isaac Luria, and many Moroccan *tzaddikim* (saints),[29] as well as at Rachel's Tomb in Bethlehem.[30]

Deceased Spirits Teach About Ethical Living In A Dream

There are a number of morality tales in the *Ma'aseh Book* in which words spoken by disembodied spirits act to emphasize certain values of traditional Jewish life and *halakhic* practice. One such story, "Of The Wicked Tax Gatherer and the Learned Rabbi Whose Bodies Were Inter-Changed at the Funeral," tells of a Jewish tax collector, known to all as a wicked man, who died on the exact same day as a pious scholar in the community. As it happened at the time of burial, a terrible confusion took place, and the two bodies were mistakenly interchanged.

The body of the tax collector was buried with great honor and accolades, while the scholar was simply whisked away to an unbecoming burial. A student of the scholar noticed the burial mix-up and was terribly upset by this incident, asking himself—a question preparing the reader for an obvious of ethical inquiry—"What kind of pious deeds had the tax collector performed in his lifetime that he should have been carried to his grave with so much honor?"[31]

In response, his teacher appeared to him that night in a dream, saying: "Do not grieve on my account, I will show you my place in Gan Eden, and I will show you, at the same time the tax collector sitting in Gehenna."

He went on to explain:

> The reason why such shame has been put upon me at my burial [is that] I once heard someone slandering a scholar and sat by quietly without protesting, though I could have done so. . .I will also tell you the good deed which the tax collector had done, which won him such honors at his burial. Once upon a time he had prepared a banquet for the governor of the town, but the governor did not come. So the tax collector took the food and distributed it among the poor of the town. Therefore God paid his reward in this world.[32]

One ethical message from this story is that the mystery of God's divine justice is not always visible from the outside. Although a person may appear one way in public—righteous or evil—it is only God who can discern the truth of a person's life and behavior. It is impossible for human folk to judge the divine scale of moral behavior: in both cases, one small deed shifted the balance and outcome of how justice was served. The function of this afterlife story is to reinforce the age-old teaching that the quality of one's deeds in life determines one's postmortem fate.

Another notable element in this story is that the dead communicate with the living through dreams. This idea is found frequently over the centuries in Jewish community life. In the Talmud, Rabbi Yehuda reported that, after doing a kindness for a deceased man, the man appeared to him in a dream thanking him for what he had done (Shabbat 152b). In the medieval period there are reports of eminent Rabbis who were said to have appeared in dreams. Rashi (1040–1105), the famous French Torah scholar and commentator revealed to his grandson correct pronunciation of the four-letter name of God. Rabbi Meir of Rothenburg (1215–1293) is reported to have appeared in a dream to help a student, interpret a confused Talmudic passage. And well-known is the legend that after being tortured and put death, Rabbi Amnon of Mainz (c. eleventh century) appeared in a dream to his teacher, Kalonymus ben Meshullam and dictated to him words of the *Unetanneh Tokef* prayer, which he had composed with his dying breath.[33] And further, in *Sefer Hasidim*, a thirteenth-century text by Rabbi Yehuda he-Hasid (Judah the Pious) there are several teachings about the importance and meaning of encountering the dead in dreams.[34] Clearly this idea was hardwired into the culture of the times, and we see this point of view reflected in the *Ma'aseh Book*.[35]

More Ethical Lessons from Deceased Spirits

Two additional stories from the *Ma'aseh Book* reinforce the essential moralistic message that how one lives life determines one's postmortem destiny.

The first, titled "Story of a Man Who Rose Alone at Night and Saw a Whole Army of Dead People Pulling Wagons Full of Other Dead People" depicts a scene of large numbers of zombie-like dead, dragging around carts of other dead people as punishment:

> One night, when the moon was shining brightly, a man was riding alone in the desert. Suddenly he saw a great number of carts full of dead people. Very much astonished, the man drew near and recognized among them a number of people who had died long ago. Then he asked these people: "Why must you draw the carts the whole night, while some of you are sitting inside?" And they said: "These carts are filled with the sins committed by us in our lifetime. We have been very free with women, therefore we must draw these carts along until we get very tired. Then they get out and we get in, and they drag the carts until they get tired, and this continues the whole night long. There are

persons appointed to beat us like beasts,
while we drag the carts. For a man is
punished in the other world for every
sin he commits." Therefore one should
beware of committing sins.[36]

The next story is "The Dead Man Who Was Driven
around a Field Which He had Unjustly Appropriated in
Life." Although only describing a single individual, not a
whole group of people, the message here is the same: you
will be punished in the world beyond for your dishonest
behavior in this life:

> Once upon a time a man lost his way
> in the great forest. In the bright moon
> light, he saw a man whom he knew to
> be dead a long time. When he wanted
> to run away, the dead man called out:
> "Be not afraid of me, I will do you no
> harm," and he made himself known
> to him. The man said: "You have been
> dead so long, what are you doing here?"
> And the dead man said: "I will tell you.
> Because I took this field away by force
> from its owner, I have no peace, for I am
> driven all night long round it."[37]

In the "The Corpse and the Torn Sleeve," there is
a postmortem encounter between a deceased spirit and
one of the men who helped prepare his body for burial,
a member of the *Hevra Kaddisha*, the Jewish burial society.
Two important rabbinic values are highlighted through

this story—1) that how one cares for the dead is of utmost importance, and 2) that a life of prayer is efficacious for bringing one a benign reward in the afterlife:

> Once upon a time there lived in the city of Worms a man called R. Bunem, who assisted in the burial of the dead. One day an old man died, and, as usual, R. Bunem accompanied the body to the grave. The next morning, when R. Bunem went to the synagogue, he saw at the door a man dressed in a shroud and with a wreath around his head. R. Bunem was frightened, for he believed he was a demon and started to run away, but the man in the shroud said him: "Do not be afraid, come here, do you not know me?" R. Bunem replied: "Are you not the man I accompanied to the grave yesterday?" Then R. Bunem said to him: "Why did you come here and how are you getting along in the other world?" He replied: "I'm getting along very well, and I'm held in high esteem in Gan Eden." R. Bunem said: "How is that? Here below we thought you were bad Jew. Tell me what pious deeds you have done to deserve respect?"
>
> The dead one replied: "I will tell you. Every morning I rose early and read my prayers and blessings with great devotion. Therefore, I now say the blessings in Gan Eden and I'm held

and in high esteem. And if you do not believe me, I will give you a sign which will convince you. When you put the shroud on me yesterday you tore one of my sleeves." Then R. Bunem said: "What does the wreath on your head mean?" He said: "It is made of good herbs of Gan Eden and keeps the evil demons from doing me harm."

Then he asked R. Bunem to mend his sleeve for he said he was shamed of the other spirits, who had whole garments, while his were torn. Then the dead man disappeared.[38]

And in the final sentences, the clear morality intent to the stories obvious:

The moral of the tale is that every man should say his prayers with devotion and it will go well with him in the other world; and moreover, one should be careful not to forget anything when dressing dead bodies.[39]

In addition to this afterlife story being a morality tale, it is interesting to note how classical images from rabbinic midrash or Talmud show up in folk-level stories. Here, the wreath on the spirit being is fully resonant with a parallel image in Talmud that states: "In the World to Come . . . the righteous sit with crowns on their head and enjoy the radiance of the *Shekhinah* [Divine Presence]" (Berakhot

17a). We will see a similar weaving together of rabbinic and kabbalistic eschatology and folk-level storytelling elsewhere in Yiddish literature.[40]

The Dybbuk of the Ma'aseh Book

In the *Ma'aseh Book*, we encounter a tale about a confused and evil spirit—a dybbuk.[41] Titled "The Dibbuk" (sic) by Moses Gaster,[42] this story is the earliest published narrative of a dybbuk possession,[43] originally "part of the hagiographic stories about Isaac Luria and his disciples,"[44] which was not published until thirty years after the *Ma'aseh Book*.[45] Found within this folk tale are many elements characteristic of dybbuk stories over the centuries.[46] But before we hear that story, some background is needed.

Underlying the notion of dybbuk, that restless malevolent entity possessing a living being, is the kabbalistic conception of *gilgul*, transmigration of souls or reincarnation. From the fourteenth century onward, *gilgul* became normative within the kabbalistic world.[47] Without going into a longer explication of the doctrine of *gilgul*—suffice it to say a person might be reincarnated for one of three reasons: 1) to make amends for sins committed; 2) to complete *mitzvoth*—divine commandments—an individual did not get to fulfill while alive; and 3) in some cases, a soul might have to incarnate for the purpose of serving the well-being of humanity and making the world a better place for others. This later idea is parallel to teachings in Buddhism on the *bodhisattva* who reincarnates "for the benefit of all sentient beings."[105]

With the proliferation of Kabbalah as a socioreligious force in the fourteenth to sixteenth centuries, the doctrine of transmigration of souls was fused with the superstitious spirit characteristic of Eastern European Jewry. According to J. H. Chajes, author of *Between Worlds: Dybbuks, Exorcists and Early Modern Judaism*, kabbalistic culture of mid-sixteenth-century Safed created a "theology of possession" in which dybbuk manifestation and possession were not uncommon at all, and frequently required extensive rituals of exorcism. Beings who were not able to successfully reincarnate became entities trapped between worlds, desperately seeking to enter the physical body of an alive person. Acting as a separate, alien personality, these possessing beings would wreak havoc in a person's life, causing mental illness, irrational outbursts, and various outrageous, inappropriate behaviors. It is this kind of situation we now read about in "The Dibbuk" of the *Ma'aseh Book*.

As the story unfolds, we immediately encounter a spirit who has taken refuge in the body of an innocent young man. When asked for his identity, the dybbuk instantly becomes agitated and dysregulated:

> An evil spirit had entered the body of a young man. Thereupon he was commanded to reveal his name or that of his wife. When they mentioned his wife he began to scream and said that his wife was an *agunah*[48], which means she had no right to marry, for he had lost his life at sea and the sages could not give her permission to remarry; that he had

requested the sages to give her permission to marry again and had given them many indications that he had been lost at sea, but they did not know where his home had been and therefore said that they could not give her permission. He was crying because she had become a harlot by reason of the fact that she could not obtain permission to marry.[49]

In many dybbuk stories, a group of learned rabbis and sages gathers around the possessed person, and proceeds to interrogate the dybbuk. Amid a barrage of chaotic cursing and swearing, the dybbuk will often confess to a variety of sins, almost always of a sexual nature. In this particular story, we meet an adulterous dybbuk who drowned and, because of his transgressions, could find no postmortem rest.

Venting and raging, the dybbuk tells his sad story:

The sages asked him why he could not rest in peace and what sins he committed, to which he replied that he had committed adultery. When the sages asked him the name of the woman with whom he sinned, he refused to tell, as she had been dead a long time and it would do no one any good if he told. "I am in the position," he said, "of the man about whom the sages say that he who is guilty of adultery should have four kinds of capital punishment

inflicted upon him. But I have not been
punished that way."[50]

Also characteristic in these stories is that the dybbuk
has access to personal information not apparent to others
in the room.[51] With bluster and perseveration, the dybbuk
points an accusing finger and reveals to all secret, illicit
sins of particular individuals in the room. In this story,
two young men are accused of sodomy, i.e. homosexuality; embarrassed and "outed," they confess:

> And while they were talking, the young
> man suddenly rose up and stood on his
> feet. The sages asked him: "Why have
> you risen up?" And the youth replied:
> "Because a great sage is coming in."
> And as they looked around, the sage
> entered, as the young man had said,
> and a company of young men followed
> him into the house to hear what was
> going on.
>
> Then the evil spirit said: "Why have
> you come in here to see me? There are
> among you some who have done the
> same fate as I and will suffer a simi-
> lar fate." The youths became terribly
> frightened. Then the evil spirit said:
> "Why are you so astounded? That
> youth yonder who is standing among
> you in white clothes, has committed
> sodomy, which is as bad as adultery."
> The youths became terrified and looked

at one another. Thereupon the young man in white clothes began screaming and said: "It is, alas, true, I am guilty." And another youth also confesses the same crime. Then one of the sages asked: "How did you know they were guilty of such a sin? The evil spirit began to laugh and said: "It is written: 'And in the hand of every man is a seal,' meaning that every man has written on his hand what deeds he has done." Then they asked him: "How can you see their hands, which are covered by their cloaks?" The evil spirit laughed and said: "I can see everywhere."[52]

This story also makes reference to the idea of reincarnation into animal bodies. The dybbuk reports first entering a cow, and then, due to close proximity to the young man, passes from an animal body to a human being:

Then they asked him how he had come to be in the young man. And he replied he had had no rest in the water, as the fish ate his body. Then his soul departed from him and entered a cow. The cow became insane, and the gentile owner sold it to a Jew who killed it, and as the youth was standing nearby, he flew straight into him.[53]

This notion of transmigration into animal bodies appeared in the thirteenth century in both *Sefer Ha-Te-munah* (1250) and *Taamei Ha-Mitzvot* (c. 1290–1300). In these texts, *gilgul* was seen as punishment for sexual acts prohibited by Torah, and thus one would be condemned to rebirth in the body of an animal.[54] Similarly, in *Shaar HaMitzvot*, Chaim Vital wrote that there are people "whose sins are so many that, after their death, they will transmigrate to animals beneath their level."[55] However, in subsequent centuries this did not emerge as the dominant view of reincarnation and does not appear at all in the Zohar, the central text of Kabbalah.

Back to the story, which reaches its conclusion with one simple sentence: "Thereupon the sages exorcised him and he left the youth and flew away."[56] In the folk-mythic style of the *Ma'aseh Book*, this story has a simple feel-good ending—no dramatic details of exorcising a resistant, angry dybbuk are recorded here. But elsewhere, as we shall see, particularly in An-sky's play, *The Dybbuk or Between Two Worlds*, exorcism can be a complex and arduous process, and not all dybbuk stories end with such an effortless dissolution of the possessing dybbuk.

Reflecting on the dybbuk of the *Ma'aseh Book* through the framework of traditional Jewish afterlife teachings: the possessing spirit of the dybbuk can be seen as a disembodied being who is not able to enter Gehenna to experience a postmortem purification process. As understood in the teachings of Kabbalah, the dybbuk is stuck in a realm referred to as *Hibbut Ha-Kever*—the Pangs of the Grave—which takes place soon after death. But most souls are able to detach from the world of materiality and move on. Whereas the dybbuk is stuck in a realm of attachment and confusion, and in desperation attempts to move on its afterlife journey by attaching itself to another being in another body. And only through exorcism, and being banished from its possessed host, is the soul of the dybbuk able to move on through the afterlife realms.

The Ma'aseh Book *as a Link in the Evolution of Jewish Afterlife Teachings*

Alongside stories of visiting spirits and lost ghosts, the *Ma'aseh Book* introduces into the legacy of Jewish afterlife teachings the motif of a malevolent possessing dybbuk. In the centuries following the heyday of medieval Kabbalah, and concomitant with the rise of Hasidism, stories of dybbukim (plural) proliferate in Yiddish literature. As we shall see below, writings on the dybbuk are interwoven into Yiddish literary fiction, and given center stage in An-sky's play *The Dybbuk or Between Two Worlds*, and subsequently in countless early modern and contemporary re-creations of this production.

4

IMAGES OF AFTERLIFE IN THE WRITINGS OF SHOLEM ALEICHEM (1859-1916)

Biographical Background

Sholem Rabinovitch, commonly known by his pseudonym Sholem Aleichem, was born in Pereyaslev, Ukraine in 1859, and spent his childhood in the shtetl of Voronokov, where he received a traditional Jewish education. His father was an unusual combination of a Hasid and a *maskil*—a devotional Jew, an enlightened intellectual, and initially a successful merchant, whose failed business venture later plunged the family into poverty. When he was still quite young, Sholem Aleichem's brother died, and soon after, just after the time of his Bar Mitzvah, his mother died in a cholera plague. These formative experiences laid the groundwork for character qualities of both curiosity and openness to change. Raised at different times by a grandparent, and then when his father re-married, by a step-mother, in early adolescence he began to seek personal solace using the written word to transform "the misfortune away from his heart."[57]

Originally, Sholem Aleichem wrote in Hebrew, and after his marriage to Olga Loyev, in 1883, he began writing in Yiddish, having his first stories and essays published that same year. At different times, his roles were that of an orphaned child, dedicated family man, teacher of Russian, a struggling rabbi and successful stockbroker, social historian and the literary mouthpiece of the poor shtetl Jew. And at the same time, over many years, he suffered through personal family tragedies, challenges to his health, commercial disasters and the cultural and political vicissitudes of the late nineteenth and early twentieth centuries.[58] His writings presented a profoundly compelling picture of Eastern European Jewish life, describing the wrenching transition from the traditional shtetl of centuries past to the dynamic and fertile reality of the modern age.[59] Authoring stories and novels, political and polemical essays and plays, he became the most renowned Yiddish author of his time throughout Eastern Europe and later in America.

After the 1905 pogrom of the first Russian revolution, Sholem Aleichem left his homeland of Eastern Europe never to return. He traveled frequently, giving literary performances throughout Europe, living at different times in Lemberg, Geneva, London, and after the outbreak of World War I, New York. The last years of his life were spent in New York, where he continued his prolific writing. In autumn 1915 he was impacted deeply by the death of his son Misha, and after that, his own health began to decline.

Sholem Aleichem died on May 13th, 1916.[60] In honor of his life and death, on the day of his burial almost all Jewish factories in New York were closed. It was reported that 150,000 to 250,000 people turned out for his funeral, said to be the largest public funeral in New York City history at that time.[61]

Sholem Aleichem's Writings on the Afterlife

Sholem Aleichem created a profound literary legacy, and his prodigious popularity did not diminish after his death, but in fact, spread well-beyond the Yiddish-speaking world. In the past century his works have been translated into English, Hebrew, and Russian, as well as most European languages, and dramatic adaptations of his stories performed by noted American, Polish, Russian, Israeli, and even Japanese theatrical troupes.[62]

Regarded during most of his life as a humorist and a popular writer for the masses, Sholem Aleichem's stories and novels have been described as some of the most optimistic works of Yiddish literature ever penned.[63] While death and madness are not absent from his writings, Sholem Aleichem depicted the Jewish cultural ambiance he saw before his eyes with "a zest for life, an unspoiled freshness, [and] an unceasing ability to renew oneself, recuperate and regenerate."[64]

Actually, unlike the other Yiddish authors examined below—Isaac Leib Peretz, S. An-sky and Isaac Bashevis Singer—Sholem Aleichem rarely wrote about themes of the afterlife and spirits of the world beyond. His world was wholly secular; he was not concerned with the exotic, mythic, and phantasmal dimensions of unseen, invisible worlds. Instead, Sholem Aleichem was "interested in the everyday life of his characters, in the prosaic conditions of their existence, in their habits, ways, and manners as they are reflected in the marketplace, at home, at gatherings, assemblies, and meetings, in times of joy and sorrow."[65] Told with a sentimental and humorous edge, his stories and novels portray an intimate insider's look at the Jewish ghetto, stretching from Eastern Europe to the Lower East Side.[66] However, one unequivocal depiction of Jewish images of postmortem survival found in the work of Sholem Aleichem appears in his *Tevye the Dairyman* stories, written between 1894 and 1916,[67] and later adapted into the Broadway production, *Fiddler on the Roof*, performed starring Zero Mostel from 1964 to 1972, and then in 1971 as a Hollywood movie with Topol, and in countless productions ever since. The story of Tevye and his daughters caricatured in *Fiddler on the Roof* has become a cultural icon in which age-old Jewish afterlife teachings manifest through the mystical other-worldly intrusions of Frume Soreh, the deceased wife of Layzer Wolf, and Golde's grandmother, Tsaytl, who visit from the realm of the dead. Although not often regarded as such, this is an enduring image of Jewish afterlife teachings that Sholem Aleichem, perhaps unknowingly, has bequeathed to our times.

Ghosts From the Beyond in Tevye the Dairyman Stories

Tevye the Dairyman is a fictional protagonist in a compilation of ten short stories, authored by Sholem Aleichem during the last twenty years of his life. Depicting an era of social and political upheaval, the Tevye tales describe the absurdity of Tevye's business dealings, the melodramatic romances of his daughters, and troublesome confrontations with Russian government officials. These stories illuminate the variegated conflicts Jews encountered as traditional life collided with modernity in late-nineteenth-century Eastern Europe.[68]

As it turns out, the content of the play and movie *Fiddler on the Roof* bears only scant resemblance to the original collection of *Tevye the Dairyman* stories. Even the name *Fiddler on the Roof* is not based on Sholem Aleichem writings, but comes from a painting by Marc Chagall, *Le Violoniste*—and a number of similar works—depicting a melancholic fiddler against the background of the roof of a tiny Russian farmhouse.[69] The *Fiddler on the Roof* storyline uses as its basis only four of the Tevye stories,[70] and in particular, the story "Today's Children" contains the famed afterlife dream scene of postmortem visitation in *Fiddler on the Roof.*

Here we shall examine the version of Tevye's dream found in the original written Sholem Aleichem story. Aleichem describes Tevye's fearful and frenetic response when first awakening out of a dream in which he encountered someone from the world beyond:

> In a word, in the middle of the night, when the whole world house was sound asleep, snoring and whistling to the dead, I suddenly sat up in bed and began to shout at the top of my voice, "Help! Help! For God's sake, help!"
>
> Everyone woke up, of course, and quickest of all my wife Golde. "My God, Tevye," she said, shaking me, "wake up! What is it? What are you screaming for?"
>
> I opened my eyes, glanced all around as though looking for someone,

and gasped in a trembling voice, "Where is she?"

"Who is she?" asks my wife. "Who are you looking for?"

"For Frume Soreh," I say. "Layzer Wolf's Frume Soreh was just here."

"You must have a fever," she says. "God help you, Tevye, Layzer Wolf's Frume Soreh passed away years ago."

"I know she did," I say. "But she was just standing here by my bed, talking to me. And she grabbed me by the throat and tried to choke me!"

"Oh, my God, Tevye," she says, "you're delirious. It was only a dream. Spit three times against the Evil Eye, tell me what you dreamed, and you'll see that it's nothing to be afraid of."[71]

Tevye is certain of his experience, and in very palpable ways felt the presence of Frume Sorah, deceased wife of Layzer Wolf, the man who had been courting Tevye's daughter, Tsaytl (named for her maternal great-grandmother). On the other hand, Golde, who represents the skepticism of modernity, is doubtful that he has really interacted with the spirit of the deceased Frume Sorah—"It was only a dream" she says. But at the same time, she is not convinced Tevye can simply ignore the dream. Her culturally bred folk-level superstition wants to protect him from harm, encouraging him to "spit three times against the Evil Eye" thus performing a very ancient practice protecting one's self against evil.[72] Here it is the evil one might encounter from a deceased spirit. But she does invite Tevye to share the dream with her. Tevye continues, and in this part of the dream there is yet another visitor from the world beyond, Golde's grandmother, Tsaytl:

> "God bless you, Golde," I say. "If it weren't for you, I would have croaked on the spot from sheer fright. Bring me a glass of water and I'll tell you my dream . . .
>
> "[N]ow listen. At first I dreamed that we were having some sort of celebration, a wedding or an engagement party, I'm not even sure which. All sorts of people were there, the rabbi too, even a band of musicians. Then a door opened and in came your Grandmother Tsaytl, God rest her soul."
>
> As soon as I mentioned her grandmother, my wife turned as white as the wall and cried out, "How did she look and what was she wearing?"
>
> "She looked," I said, "like your enemies should, as yellow as wax, and she was wearing something white, it must have been a funeral shroud . . . 'Mazel tov!' she says to me. 'I'm so pleased to hear that you've chosen a fine young man for your Tsaytl, your eldest daughter who is named for me. He's called Motl Komzoyl, after my cousin Mordechai, and he an excellent fellow, even if he is a tailor.'"[73]

In Tevye's dream, Golde's grandmother Tsaytl appears and, from here, recommends a husband for her great-granddaughter and namesake, Tevye's daughter Tsaytl. She insists it must be Motl Komzoyl, the tailor, and not Layzer Wolf, the butcher, who is destined to marry the young girl.

Next in Tevye's dream vision we see that Layzer Wolf's deceased wife Frume Soreh appears, and likewise she is convinced that Tsaytl should not and will not marry Layzer Wolf. She is furious that marriage to him is even being considered:

> "Right you are, Grandma," I say. "But what exactly do you propose that we do about Layzer Wolf? I hope you realize that I've given my word . . ."
>
> No sooner had I said that then I looked up—your grandmother Tsaytl was gone! Now Frume Soreh was standing in her place, and this is what she said to me: "Reb Tevye! I have always thought that you were a learned, honorable Jew; would you kindly explain to me, then, how you can let your daughter take over my house, sit in my chairs, carry my keys, walk around in my coats, put on my jewelry, and wear my pearls?" "But why blame me?" I say to her. "That's what your Layzer Wolf wants." "Layzer Wolf?" she says. "Layzer Wolf will come to no good end, while as for your daughter Tsaytl—I feel sorry for

your daughter, Reb Tevye, because she
won't live out three weeks with him.
If she does, I promise that I'll come to
her in person the next night, and throt-
tle her, like this." And with those very
words, Frume Soreh grabbed me by the
throat and began to squeeze so hard
that if you hadn't waked me when you
did I'd be in the world to come now.[74]

Evidenced in this story is that the dead not only
intervene, but can see what takes place among the living.
We can imagine Frume Soreh being able to witness her
marital replacement using the possessions she left behind.
And she would have none of that.

In response to the dream, Tevye and Golde are
frightened off by Frume Soreh's threats of revenge, and
persuaded by Grandma Tsaytl's recommendation of a
husband for their daughter:

May the butcher [Layzer Wolf] have
black dreams himself! He should break
a hand and a foot before anything happens to Motl Komzoyl's little finger,
even if he is a tailor! Believe me, if he's
named after my cousin Mordechai, he
doesn't have a tailor's soul. And if my
grandmother, may she rest in peace, has
taken the trouble of coming all the way
from the next world to wish us a mazel
tov, we'd better say mazel tov ourselves.
It should only turn out for the best.

They should have lots of happiness,
amen and amen.[75]

Through Sholem Aleichem's stories, we see in this
dream the worldview of late medieval/early modern
Judaism, in which the living and the dead interface with
each other. The dead are not in a static realm, gone
and forgotten, but through dreams and visions they
find active ways to interact with the living. Even though
Sholem Aleichem was originally trained as a rabbi, his
secular writings do not attempt to portray the religiosity
of his family and culture of origin. And yet, nonetheless,
this famous scene of Tevye's dream leaves a legacy of a
Jewish world in which there is a life after death, and those
beings who have made the transition from physical life
to the world beyond remain in contact with the world of
the living. These ideas represent classical Jewish afterlife
thought replicating ideas found in biblical, rabbinic and,
kabbalistic traditions.

From Yiddish Fiction to the Yiddish Stage, the Silver Screen, Broadway, and the World

The dramatized tale of Tevye and his family life in
the Eastern European shtetl has become ubiquitous in
the contemporary world, even more than in Sholem
Aleichem's time. One could say that *Fiddler on the Roof*
brought the works of Sholem Aleichem to life, even
more than Sholem Aleichem brought *Fiddler on the Roof*
to life. Although he wrote a stage adaptation of the Tevye
stories, it was never produced prior to his death, and it is

likely that while he was alive Sholem Aleichem had never even heard of the play, *Fiddler on the Roof.*

It was only after Sholem Aleichem's death that Maurice Schwartz, founder of Yiddish Art Theatre in New York, produced Sholem Aleichem's play adaptation of the Tevye stories, in 1919; and twenty years later, just as World War II was breaking out in 1939, Schwartz released the film *Tevye*, which many years later became the first non-English language picture selected for preservation by the National Film Registry.[76]

From the 1960s onward, Sholem Aleichem's portrayal of shtetl life reached a global audience with the Broadway production of *Fiddler on the Roof*—the first musical in theatre history to surpass three thousand performances—followed by the 1971 English-language film version. Subsequently, theatrical versions of *Fiddler* were produced in Soviet Russia and Israel, and today one can find on YouTube Japanese, Korean, Hindi, and Hungarian versions of *Fiddler on the Roof.* What is more, as Jeremy Dauber notes: "Closer to home, high school marching band performances and at least one sock puppet parody nestle side by side with a seemingly infinite number of shaky recordings of high school and community theater productions."[77] Everybody loves the songs that made *Fiddler on the Roof* famous!

Through the proliferation of artistic creations—in writing, theater, film, song, and, more recently, the internet—the stories of Tevye and his daughters have moved from the confines of shtetl life in the Pale of the Settlement to an international, multicultural stage. Depicting the archetypal struggle between the past and the future, between old traditions and the emergence of modern ideas, Sholem Aleichem's Tevye stories, as portrayed in the kaleidoscopic panorama of worldwide *Fiddler on the Roof* productions, have been described as "arguably the most popular and powerful representations of Jewish life to the world at large since the closing of the biblical canon."[78]

And included in this portrayal of Jewish life is the age-old Jewish belief that consciousness survives bodily death, and that beings from the world beyond can and do find their way to commune with the living. As a literary depiction of Jewish views of the afterlife emerging out of Eastern European Yiddish culture, this is the message that Sholem Aleichem communicates to our age through *Tevye the Dairyman* stories and *Fiddler on the Roof*.

5

IMAGES OF AFTERLIFE IN THE WRITINGS OF I.L PERETZ (1851-1915)

Biographical Background

Isaac Leib (Yitzchok Leybush) Peretz, one of the great Yiddish poets and authors of all time, was born in 1852, in Zamosc, Poland, a small, southeastern Poland city that was known as a regional center of learning and trade. Raised in a respected middle-class family, he received traditional training in Hebrew and private tutoring in German and Russian. A child prodigy, at the age of fifteen Peretz discovered a library of three thousand volumes. The story is told that a wealthy community member in his town collected a vast library, which was put in storage when his financial fortunes were reversed. Peretz somehow got access to a key to that library and voraciously read everything he could get his hands on—a vast array of Polish, German, and Russian literature.[79] Trained as a lawyer, from 1877 to 1888 Peretz practiced law in Zamosc until his license was revoked for radical socialist activities. After relocating to Warsaw in 1890, Peretz established contacts with Jewish literary circles, and began publishing his poetry in Yiddish. Over the next two decades he emerged as the central figure in Yiddish-speaking Warsaw, becoming one of the dominant influences on the spread of Yiddish literary culture throughout the Jewish world. For years, there was seldom a Jewish soirée in major European cities that took place, without readings from Peretz's works.[80]

Many streams of influence can be seen in Peretz's life: from Hasidic romanticism, to enlightenment and Haskalah rationalism, from radical socialism, early Zionism and Jewish nationalism, to Yiddishist Jewish culture—which he himself helped create and proliferate. Peretz was not rigid or fixed in his beliefs, and over the course of his lifetime many changing loyalties and affinities were expressed through the wide swath of his literary creativity. Always attuned to the avant-garde literary trends of his era, Peretz produced a prolific body of work—poetry, drama, essays, literary reviews, and, most notably, short stories.[81]

In his writings Peretz integrated the emerging future of modernity with spiritual depths of the Jewish past. On one hand, he was both a social critic and a realist in his writing style. Supportive of the socialist labor movement and rejecting of Jewish traditionalism, for Peretz and his contemporaries "religious observances and ancient rituals . . . [were seen] as a moat of stagnant waters separating the walled Jewish fortress from the wide world beyond."[82] As an "artist of the Jewish soul,"[83] Peretz wrote stories and folk tales portraying "everyday experiences, with problems of the average man, the struggle for bread, the trials of marriage, the joys and cares of parenthood, the alternation of births, feasts and funerals."[84]

And yet, on the other hand, Peretz was also a romanticist with a nostalgic appreciation of bygone days of Jewish spiritual wisdom. In depicting the inner essence of life, he drew from the legacy of Hasidism, authoring tales of mystics, Rabbis, and ordinary folk experiencing numinous sojourns into transcendental heavens and invisible realms of wisdom and light.[85] Ever "an optimist who believed in the inevitability of progress through enlightenment, he infused many of his stories with the age-old Jewish vision of Messianic hope and redemption."[86]

Toward the end of his lifetime, Peretz was more reserved than many of his contemporaries in support of the Russian Revolution of 1905. He was concerned that the universalist vision of the Revolution would preclude an appreciation of Jewish uniqueness of both language and cultural expression. Continuing his literary pursuits to the very end of his days, Peretz died of a heart attack on April 3rd, 1915. He was buried in Warsaw, with over 100,000 people attending his funeral.[87]

In the year after his death, Yiddish writers in the United States formed a literary association named after Peretz. Similarly in the early twentieth century, Jewish communities in North America, South America, and Europe continued to honor his legacy, naming schools, libraries, streets, and organizations for Peretz, in acknowledgement of his pivotal role as a progenitor of modern Jewish cultural creativity.[88]

I.L. Peretz's Writings on the Afterlife

The unique style of Peretz's Yiddish fiction combined psychological caricature and social satire with motifs and themes of the Jewish spirit. Below, we shall look at two stories of Peretz depicting traditional Jewish concepts on the afterlife, interwoven with the worldview of early modernity.

"What is the Soul? The Story of a Young Man" is one of Peretz's earliest prose works, published in 1890. This story contains a series of reflections on the nature of the soul and life after death, seen through the eyes of a child who, over the years of the story, is developing into a young man. While neither a very well-written, nor theologically-sophisticated story, "What is the Soul?" depicts questions and problems thinking about soul and afterlife within the context of rationalism and early modernity. Throughout, the story is infused with a cornucopia of traditional Jewish motifs of the afterlife.

The second story, "Bontshe Shvayg" is one of the most beloved stories in all of Yiddish literature. Written in 1894, this story tells the tale of the death a simple man—Bontshe Shvayg—who led an inconsequential life and dies an ignoble, quiet death. Yet, as Peretz so richly portrays, in the heavenly realms Bontshe Shvayg's death is of great consequence, and he is welcomed into the world beyond with great fanfare.

Lush with traditional rabbinic and kabbalistic images of postmortem judgment, both this story and "What is the Soul?—The Story of a Young Man"[89] demonstrate how Yiddish literature integrated classical Jewish understandings of the afterlife with the emerging intellectual and sociopolitical worldview of the early modern era.

"What is the Soul? The Story of a Young Man"— Postmortem Survival Meets Rationalist Thought

Published in 1890, "What is the Soul? The Story of a Young Man" tells a tale, in the inquiring voice of a young boy whose father has just died. "I remember, as in a dream . . . a small, thin man with a pointed beard . . . lying sick in bed," begins the story; and soon, "I was told that my father had died."[90] The boy continues his narration: "The next day I didn't recognize our house, straw lay strewn on the floor, the mirror was turned around to face the wall, and my mother was sitting in her stocking feet on a small stool on the floor."[91]

What Peretz describes here are familiar images of Jewish ritual practice—covered mirrors and shoeless mourners sitting on low stools in a shivah house—and the straw on the floor, although not contemporary practice, harkens back to when the deceased, immediately after a death, was placed upon the ground on top of a light bed of straw.[92] (In some Orthodox communities this practice of putting a dead body on the ground immediately after death is still carried out, although without the straw.)

The young child, overwhelmed by what he is seeing, is told his father has died, and instructed "that if I did a good job of saying the Kaddish, his soul would fly straight to heaven."[93]

Contained within this seemingly innocent statement to a young boy is a major theological assertion of medieval Judaism, the idea that a child reciting the memorial Kaddish prayer for a deceased parent has spiritual efficacy to redeem a soul from postmortem sufferings of Gehenna.[94] This idea of Kaddish being a way of connecting the living bereaved and the soul of the deceased is lost to modernity. If people do choose to say Kaddish for a deceased loved one, they think of it in psychological terms as a self-soothing bereavement ritual, which it can be. But the idea of a transcendent connection with a loved one in the afterlife, suggested here, is lost to contemporary Jewish life.

The story continues: The young boy imagines his father's soul as a bird.[95] And once, while walking home from school accompanied by the teacher's assistant he sees several low-flying birds and with joyous delight declares: "Souls are flying, souls are flying!" In a flash the assistant admonishes the young boy's view of death and the world beyond: "'You foolish boy,' he said to me, 'those are ordinary birds.'"[96]

The teacher's assistant, as the voice of modernity and rationalism, rejected and collapsed a mythic, multi-dimensional view of the universe into little more than the phenomenal and observable world—which is exactly what the Haskalah did!

The young boy, now experiencing inner conflict, asks his own mother: "How can you tell the difference between a soul and an ordinary bird?"[97]

This is the existential angst of the post-Renaissance mind which asks: "Can I trust my perceptions of the non-visible world, or is it my imagination making things up?" The young child desperately wants to know if he can really perceive his deceased father's soul.

At fourteen, the young boy had another teacher, Zorakh Pinch, named for his habit of helping students learn Talmud by pinching them "without mercy." This teacher communicated a radically different view of afterlife. "'The body . . . is only dust and ashes . . . And what is the soul?' asks the young boy. 'Something spiritual!'" the teacher answered.

In a state of thirsting inquiry, the young boy is left reflecting on this age-old question "What is spiritual?"[98]

But as yet, there is no answer, only more questions. As the story unfolds, the boy is struggling to discern the difference between body and soul.

One day, continuously tortured by his teacher's unrelenting, sadistic pinching, the young boy cries out to his dead father: "Dear Father! Take vengeance on Zorakh Pinch! Lord in Heaven, what does he want from my soul?!" But then again, ponders the young boy: "I had forgotten that he pinched only my body."

Body and soul are separate, and the relationship between the two, at least for the young boy, is not clear at all. Thus far, there is no answer to the question of "what is the soul?" The existential malaise of the young boy, mirroring the angst of the skeptical rationalist mind of modernity, has not yet found peace.

But in rare moments, when Zorakh Pinch closed the Talmud, proclaimed a holiday, and began telling his students wonder-filled stories, the young boy could see his teacher become a different person.

Next, with Peretz introducing another element of age-old rabbinic and kabbalistic theology into this story, the boy reports that: "Zorakh Pinch told us how the Almighty chooses a soul from His Treasury and blows it into a body. And I imagined that in the Almighty's treasury the souls were laid out like the merchandise in my mother's shop, in all kind of boxes—red, green, white, blue—and tied up with string."[99]

The boy's imagining is reflective of traditional rabbinic and kabbalistic teachings on a notion of "treasury of souls," referred to as *otzar* or *tzror hahayyim*—the source or the bundle of life. The Zohar (I, 66a; II, 150a) teaches that souls of all living beings have bodily garments while in this world, but don ethereal supernal garments in the postmortem "storehouse" or "treasury of souls" from whence all souls originate and ultimately return after death.[100] The teacher goes on, as Peretz now draws from another stratum of rabbinic midrash:

> "'And when God,' the teacher told us, 'chooses a soul and decrees that it must enter the sinful world, it trembles and cries. Afterward an angel comes to it inside the mother's belly and teaches it the entire Torah. But when it comes time to be born, the angel gives it a fillip under the nose, and it forgets everything it has learned.'"[101]

This exact teaching is found in a unique medieval visionary midrash, *Seder Yetzirat HaVlad* (*The Formation of the Embryo*), which chronicles the fetal life of a soul, and takes as a given that there is a pre-birth consciousness in the womb.[102]

According to *Seder Yetzirat HaVlad*:

> The Holy Blessed One places [a soul] against its will into the womb of its mother. He posts there two angels who guard him that he should not fall out, and they put a burning candle upon his head. And he looks and can see from the beginning of the world to its end.
>
> One of the angels guides the soul from morning until evening, and shows

it every place which his foot will tread,
and the place where it will be buried.
After this . . . he places it back again in
the womb of its mother and sustains the
child in the womb of its mother for nine
months.

At the end of that time the same
angel says "Come forth, for the time has
come to go forth into the world.'" The
angel touches him under the nose and
puts out the candle over his head, and
brings him out against his will, and he
forgets everything he saw.[103]

The unnamed orphan boy has not yet come to discern what exactly is the nature of the soul, but through
his teachers he has been exposed to intellectual skepticism, rabbinic mind-body dualism,[104] the existence of a
storehouse of souls,[105] and angelic presences in the womb.
Clearly, Peretz is drawing from many strata of Jewish
eschatology.

In continuing his education, the young one is assigned
a tutor for writing lessons, a man who is "a great freethinker in the town [whom] the neighbors didn't trust
. . . to keep the dietary laws."[106] And, along with this
enlightened, Haskalah-educated Jew, the following year
he is taught by yet another teacher, Reb Yoyzl, who "had
been the agent of one of the great Hasidic rabbis."[107]
With anticipation we might predict these two very different streams of Jewish thought will eventually collide.

Reb Yoyzl, in conversations with the boy spoke of
"very great souls that come from beneath the Throne of

Glory."[108] Explicating the quintessential Jewish philosophy of suffering, reward and punishment, Reb Yoyzl declared:

> "But the main thing . . . relates to suffering. No soul is ever lost; they must all return to their original level, where they were before they descended into this world—all souls are cleansed solely through suffering. The Creator in His great mercy sends suffering so that we remember that we are only flesh and blood, broken vessels, insignificant. At a mere glance of His, we disintegrate and become as the dust of the earth. But in the next world the souls are cleansed." Then [said the boy] he told me what is done to all poor souls in the seven departments of [Gehenna].[109]

In few words Peretz summarizes central Jewish ideas of the afterlife—that souls are divinely created, cleansed through life's suffering, and purified in Gehenna.

Influenced by what he was taught, notions of postmortem reward and punishment filtered into the young boy's consciousness. At night he dreamed of heavenly angels catching pure souls, as white as snow, returning from this world, and black angels scrubbing dirty souls piled into a frozen sea, and then boiled in "huge black pots lit by the fires of hell." As the dirt is squeezed from their souls, in painful anguish, they howl from one end of the universe to the other. And in this dream the young boy sees the blackened soul of his "freethinker" tutor, and an angel sternly warns him "If you follow in his ways [of liberal, non-traditional living and being], your soul will be washed until it is lost in the tortures of hell!"[110]

When he shares this dream with his tutor, he is ridiculed: "He said that dreams were foolish; he paid no attention to such things."[111] But on the other hand, in hearing the dream his mother asks if he had seen his father in the afterlife realms, and he responds "No!" "'What a pity! What a pity!' she said, disappointed. 'He surely would have given you a message for me.'"[112]

With masterful wordsmithery, in this dream Peretz combines traditional images from rabbinic and medieval midrashic texts portraying the nature of Gehenna, with social commentary highlighting the tension between tradition and modernity. In the mother's questions about the dream, once again the idea that the living and the dead commune through dreams comes through. But the diametrically opposed response of the young boy's tutor depicts early modern rationalist rejection of the ideas of afterlife survival of souls, and the individual psyche or soul as a receptor of otherworldly communication.

Through the young boy's dream, and how those around him respond, Peretz paints a crystalline picture of the conflict between Kabbalah and, between—on one hand—ancient belief in survival of consciousness after death and the interconnection between the realms of the living and the dead, and—on the other hand—the emerging *Weltanschauung* of modernity denying and rejecting belief in afterlife, angels, dreams, and all forms of non-rational knowing.

As the story continues: by the age of sixteen, matchmakers were already considering marriage options for the adolescent boy. As he continued to study Talmud, Maimonides, Tosaphot and other commentators, nonetheless his unflagging question "What is the soul?" persisted. He was even taunted and bullied by friends, called "soul-boy" and as he reported "Day and night I suffered."[113]

A girl named Gitele caught the fancy of the boy, and one day he asked of her: "'They say, Gitele, that you are smart. Please tell me what sort of thing is a soul?'"[114] At first, all she could say was 'I certainly don't know.'"

But then Peretz delivers what becomes the *piéce de résistance* of this story, and the ultimate movement towards resolution of our narrator-protagonist's existential inquiry.

> "But suddenly she became sad, and her eyes began to fill with tears. 'I remember,' she said to me, 'that when my mother, may she rest in peace, was alive, my father always said that she was his soul . . . They loved each other so much!'"[115] [And with no hesitation, he responded:] "I don't know what came over me, but at that moment I clasped her hand and said, trembling, 'Gitele, would you be my soul?' She answered very softly, 'Yes!'"[116]

As the story winds down (with some literary disappointment), Peretz shifts from the philosophical to the romantic, the boy has found his *bashert*, his destined love, and she becomes the soul he has been searching. And while his mother was unsatisfied with his choice, in the middle of the night the boy once again entered the world beyond in a dream state encountering his deceased father who, this time, sent along greetings to the boy's mother, saying he approved of his son's forthcoming marriage to Gitele. And with the words, "That is how I acquired a new soul," the story comes to an end.[117]

"What is the Soul?—The Story of a Young Man" is not written as a religious text on life after death, but it many ways it functions as such. Peretz weaves together traditional Jewish eschatological motifs with the intellectual worldview of the Enlightenment. This kind of intellectual skepticism as to whether or not a soul exists, and whether one can communicate with those in the world beyond, appears for the first time in the development of Jewish thought. With modernity this reticence to believe in postmortem survival slowly becomes part of the emerging worldview that eventually leads to the loss of Jewish afterlife traditions in the twentieth century.

"Bontshe Shvayg"—Bontshe the Silent One: Jewish Eschatology and the Cry for Social Justice

Influenced by nineteenth-century socialism, in his beloved and famous story of "Bontshe Shvayg," Peretz expresses his concern for the lives of the oppressed, suffering masses of Eastern Europe. Although Peretz's intention in this story is to critique poverty and social injustice, through literary use of traditional of imagery of postmortem judgment, drawn from rabbinic midrash and Kabbalah, this story is a wonderful portrayal of ancient Jewish afterlife teachings.

"Here on earth the death of Bontshe Shvayg made no impression. Try asking who Bontshe was, how he lived, what he died of . . . and no one can give you an answer. For all you know he might have starved to death."[118] With these words Peretz begins to tell the tale of the death and postmortem experiences of Bontshe Shvayg, a simple and insignificant man — much like Leo Tolstoy's Ivan Illych[119] — depicted as unexceptional, commonplace, and nondescript, who lived a life at once ordinary and terrible.[120]

For Peretz, Bontshe Shvayg, Bontshe the Silent, is the impoverished and voiceless invisible Everyman. Born in silence, he lived in silence and died in silence, "like a shadow he passed through this world."[121] Demonstrating his rich understanding of traditional Jewish texts, here Peretz uses an image from Psalm 144:3-4: "O Lord, what is man, that You should take care about him? . . . Man is like a breath; his days are like a passing shadow." Used in funeral and Yizkor liturgy this Psalm speaks of the frail nature of human life, that all beings are destined to die, like wisps of wind we pass through life for a short period of time and then disappear from the world. And as for Bontshe Shvayg, "alone he lived and alone he died,"[122] and the insignificance of his life was only surpassed by the conspicuous insignificance of his death.

> While Bontshe lived, his feet left no tracks in the mud; when he died, the wind blew away the wooden sign marking his grave. The gravedigger's wife found it some distance away and used it to boil potatoes. Do you think that three days after Bontshe was dead anyone

knew where he lay? There was not even
a gravestone for a future antiquarian to
unearth and mouth the name of Bontshe Shvayg one last time.[123]

But in the heavenly realms, Bontshe's death was
announced with great fanfare, an occasion for euphoric
celebration. Describing the afterlife adventures of Bontshe Shvayg, Peretz portrays a traditional postmortem
scene weaving together classical rabbinic and kabbalistic
afterlife imagery: "A blast of the Messiah's horn sounded
in all seven heavens: 'Bontshe Shvayg has passed away!
Bontshe has been summoned to his Maker!' the most
exalted angels with the brightest wings informed each
other in mid-flight. A joyous din broke out in paradise."[124]

The welcoming scene here is grand. The shofar that
will herald Messianic redemption resounds throughout
all seven realms of Gan Eden. Bontshe is greeted at the
heavenly gates by Father Abraham, escorted by two
accompanying angels. These are historic Midrashic
images: Sifre Deuteronomy 10:67a speaks of seven realms
of Gan Eden; in the medieval Midrashic text Gedulat
Moshe, Moses is shown a vision of Gan Eden, where
he meets Abraham; and the choirs of welcoming angels
are found in Pesikta Rabbati 49:8 and Zohar I, 98a; I,
100a.[125] Peretz is chronicling the heavenly adventures of
Bontshe Schvayg with rich and extensive medieval afterlife imagery.

Next, we encounter the spectacle of a Heavenly
Tribunal, *Beit Din shel Malah.* Although Bontshe's heavenly reward is a forgone conclusion—"Everyone knows
that's only a formality. The prosecution doesn't have a

leg to stand on. The whole business will be over in five minutes"[126]—nonetheless his sins and virtues must be evaluated. As the courtroom scene unfolds, with details of a judicial process reflecting Peretz's training as a lawyer, Bontshe is nervous. Ushered before the Heavenly Tribunal, "he was scared out of his wits,"[127] as the records of his deeds, and the quality of his character are chronicled. This is a perfect iteration of the postmortem life review and judgment integral to Jewish afterlife teachings in Apocrypha (2 Enoch 44:5; 3 Enoch 26:12), rabbinic literature (M. Avot. 4:29; Taan. 11a), and Kabbalah (Zohar I, 79a, III, 126b).

The courtroom trial proceeds. "'The name of Bontshe Shvayg, Bontshe the Silent,' the counsel was saying, 'fit him like a tailored suit . . . Not once in his whole life . . . did he complain to God or to man. Not once did he feel a drop of anger or cast an accusing glance at heaven."[128] With never-ending tragedies of bad luck, incessant hardships, bereavement, degradation, meager employment and the indignities of poverty; with a drunk for a father, no friends or schoolmates, no proper schooling, barely any clothes to wear, and abandoned by his wife, abused by his son—in spite of it all, "he bore it all in silence . . . at no time did he ever say a word."[129]

The counsel for the defense went on:

> [Even as he lay dying,] he kept silent when the doctor would not examine him without half a ruble in advance and when the orderly wanted five kopecks to change his dirty sheets . . . He kept silent

when he died. Not one word against
God. Not one word against man.[130]

With the life review complete, the defense rested.
Bontshe trembled, knowing the prosecution was yet to
present its case before the Heavenly Tribunal. He waited
with anxious anticipation, until the prosecuting attorney
declared: "Gentleman . . . *he* kept silent. I will do the
same."[131] In a stunning reversal of fortune, the Heavenly
Tribunal determined they could "pass no judgment" on
Bontshe Shvayg. His long-suffering life of silence was
sufficient in itself, and in response Bontshe received his
heavenly reward:

> "There, in the world below, no one
> appreciated you . . . There, in the World
> of Deceit, your silence went unre-
> warded. Here in the World of Truth, it
> will be given its full due. The Heavenly
> Tribunal can pass no judgment on you.
> It is not for us to determine your portion
> of paradise. Take what you want it is all
> yours!"[132]

Emotionally overwhelmed by the verdict of the
Heavenly Tribunal, "Bontshe Shvayg looked up for the
first time. His eyes were blinded by rays of light that
streamed at him from all over. Everything glittered, glis-
tened, blazed with light: the walls, the benches, the angels,
the judges."[133] Looking around, Bontshe is in awe of the
multitude of angels present before him—Peretz's imagery
is suggestive of the repeatedly used phrase "myriads of

angels" in rabbinic (Yalkut Shimoni, Bereshit 20) and medieval midrash (Midrash Gedulat Moshe, 9, 11).

Still insecure, uncertain, "he cast his dazed eyes down again. 'Truly?, he asked, happy but abashed. 'Why, of course!' the judge said . . . 'All heaven belongs to you. Ask for anything you wish; you can choose what you like.'"[134]

Evidenced here is a transformation of classical rabbinic eschatology and the emergence of a post-Enlightenment theology. Even though Peretz is using traditional Jewish imagery of postmortem judgment, notions of afterlife here reflect new cultural parameters; we have come a long way from rabbinic notions of God as the progenitor and bestower of reward and punishment. Here, it is not a transcendent God who provides postmortem judgment for the soul of the deceased. Instead, God's role is now allocated to the high judge of the Heavenly Tribunal.

Even more, in the spirit of Enlightenment individualism, Bontshe Shvayg himself is allowed to choose his due reward. In a literary twist that has made this story a beloved Yiddish tale for generations, when asked what he wants as his just reward: "'Well then,' smiled Bontshe, 'what I would like most of all is a warm roll with fresh butter every morning.'"[135] In this humble action of Bontshe Shvayg, Peretz presents a social critique of the disempowered shtetl Jew. A poor, impoverished victim of class oppression, when given unbounded options for divine reward, Bontshe Shvayg envisions little more than a warm roll and butter on his table for breakfast. The cultural and political life of his environment has left him with a skewed and retracted view of the possible. This is what Peretz is conveying in this story.

In response to Bontshe's request: "The judges and angels hung their heads in shame, the prosecutor laughed."[136] For Peretz, the fate of Bontshe the Silent and of the Eastern European Jewish masses are identical: a fate imbued with sadness, and a despair that resonates in the supernal realms. Although he has used a full spate of afterlife imagery throughout this story, his sociopolitical intent is to portray the 'Everyman' of Bontshe the Silent as a downtrodden soul crushed by class injustice.

In telling his tale of the hapless Bontshe Shvayg, Peretz presents a complete scenario of divine afterlife judgment, based on classical teachings of Jewish tradition. Even as the era of modernity, secularism, socialist thought, and Enlightenment rationalism emerges on the cultural horizon of Eastern European Jewish life, Judaism's ancient notions of divine reward and punishment in the afterlife persist in the literary legacy of Isaac Leib Peretz and Bontshe Shvayg. However, within a matter of decades, as Jews left the old shtetl life behind to build a new life in America, teachings about life after death became increasingly irrelevant to the social concerns of subsequent generations. Slowly the Jewish understanding of survival of consciousness after death was replaced by the Haskalah notion that Judaism believes in the life and the living, and the afterlife means one lives on through one's descendants.[137]

6

S. AN-SKY (1863-1920)
AND *THE DYBBUK*—
GILGUL GONE AWRY

Biographical Background

Shloyme Zanvl Rappoport, later known by his pseudonym S. An-sky, was born October 15th, 1863 to a poor
family in Vitebsk, Russia [now in Belarus], a center of
Chabad Hasidism and home to one of the great yeshivas
of Eastern European Orthodoxy. A Talmudic prodigy in
his youth, over the course of his lifetime An-sky was influenced by a commingling of traditional Judaism, Hasidic
mysticism, writings of Haskalah, revolutionary activism
of socialism, as well as Russian and Yiddish literature.
At seventeen the young Shloyme Zanvl lost his faith and,
feeling estranged from the Jews, taught himself Russian in
order to function in the broader society. With wanderlust
in his character, he traveled to many European cities,
working at a variety of occupations including as a tutor
of Russian, a bookbinder, and a miner; during the intense
political activist phase of his life, he worked as a Russian
journalist and socialist propagandist; and toward the end
of his life, he served as a researcher of Jewish folklore, an
author, and a playwright.[138]

At the close of the eighteenth century, An-sky got involved with the Jewish Labor Bund, and in 1905, after encountering Zionist youth groups in Geneva, became supportive of the nascent Jewish nationalist cause.[139] After reading I.L. Peretz's collective writings in 1905, An-sky was exhilarated when he discovered a European sensibility expressed through Yiddish. This motivated his return to writing in Yiddish, after a two-decade hiatus. Subsequently, in the last decades of his life, An-sky, like Peretz, and his later contemporary, Martin Buber, was a neo-Hasid, inspired by the mystical tales of Hasidism, yet firmly planted in secular enlightenment thought and socialist politics.[140]

During his lifetime An-sky produced a wide assortment of articles, stories, folktales, poetry, novellas, memoirs, ethnographies, war reports, socialist propaganda pamphlets, and plays. His posthumous works comprise fifteen volumes, and this likely represents only a fraction of his literary output.[141] But his play *The Dybbuk or Between Two Worlds* left an enduring and widespread influence on Yiddish literature.

A story of possession by a discarnate soul, or dybbuk, that has not found peace, An-sky's *The Dybbuk* was authored between 1913 and 1914. It was originally written in Russian because during World War I, a Yiddish play would have never been approved by the local censor. An-sky later translated *The Dybbuk* into Yiddish and spent the last years of his life negotiating for the staging of his play.[142]

On November 8th, 1920, An-sky died in Warsaw, never having seen *The Dybbuk* performed on stage. But having achieved fame as a playwright in Jewish Warsaw, upon his death, local Yiddish theaters went dark as a sign of mourning.[143] One month after An-sky's death, following the traditional thirty-day mourning period, a Yiddish version of *The Dybbuk* was performed in Warsaw. Capturing the Jewish cultural anxiety about the decline of traditional religion, the play was an instant success.[144] A Hebrew version translated by Hayim Nahman Bialik was staged in Moscow two years later, and in 1937 the Yiddish film classic *The Dybbuk* (*Der Dibuk*) was filmed in Poland.[145] Produced widely in different cultures, contexts and media, since then, there is a timeless element in *The Dybbuk* story that has captivated the Jewish psyche for almost a century since it first premiered in Warsaw.[146]

Background to the Writing of The Dybbuk

Various cultural influences and Jewish sources[147] inspired An-sky's writing of *The Dybbuk*, including reading reports of dybbuk possession, romanticized attachment to tales of wonder-working Hasidic Rebbes, awareness of the antinomian tendencies of Sabbatean writing[148] (which impact his main protagonist in the play), and, most notably, his involvement in a major Eastern European Jewish ethnographic expedition.

From 1911 to 1914 An-sky worked as head of the Baron Horace Guenzburg Jewish Ethnographic Expedition. Traveling from village to village interviewing men and women in the shtetls of the Volhynia and Podolia regions of Ukraine, the Expedition chronicled Jewish folkloristic practices that were slowly vanishing with the advance of modernity.

As Ruthie Abelovich writes:

> Equipped with state-of-the-art technology of the time (a camera and a phonograph) they recorded thousands of Yiddish songs, folktales, and proverbs; took two thousand photographs; and gathered hundreds of historical documents and samples of Jewish material culture, including, attire, religious articles, and even recipes of traditional food.[149]

In addition, the Expedition gathered responses to more than 2,500 ethnographic questions, including a series of queries on death and dying such as the following:

> Is there a belief among you that if a dying man's bed contains iron, his death throes will be prolonged?
>
> Is there a belief among view that when the soul departs it is forbidden to stand opposite in the dying man's bed, because that is when the Angel of Death appears wielding a sword?
>
> Why [upon a person's death] must one spill out all the water from his house and all the surrounding houses?
>
> Do you know any stories about a corpse that was left unattended and disappeared?
>
> How does one ask forgiveness of the dead? Who is the first to ask forgiveness?

What is one accustomed to say? . . .

Is there a belief among you that when the last shovel hits the earth, the dead man forgets everything?

Do you believe that when you meet it dead man you should strike him a blow in an offhand manner in order to make him disappear?

Do you know any stories about a dead person being brought before a rabbinical court?[150]

One question in the ethnographic inventory focused specifically on stories about disembodied spirits: "Do you know any stories about a dead person's soul that finds no rest and turned into a dybbuk and enters a living person?"[151] From responses assembled, An-sky amassed a large collection of dybbuk tales, and these stories became foundational material inspiring him to write a play with dybbuk possession as a central theme. This notion of a possessing spirit, which had emerged out of the kabbalistic doctrine of *gilgul*—reincarnation, entered the folk level of community life in Eastern Europe in the seventeenth and eighteenth centuries. An-sky having read and heard first and second-hand reports of dybbuks, garnered mythic data and vital thematic content for his unique play.

The inspiration for An-sky's four-act play emerged from his travels. The people he met, the places he visited, and his encounters with the cultural memory of the 1648 Chmielnicki massacres in Ukraine served as a historical backdrop for the theatrical production. As a secular Jew, An-sky's primary goal was not to primarily to illuminate kabbalistic teachings on afterlife and the doctrine of *gilgul*, even though they underlie his story of dybbuk possession and exotic exorcism rituals. Neither Torah exegesis, nor midrash, nor philosophy, *The Dybbuk, or Between Two Worlds* is a play, a unique genre of afterlife literature radically different than the sacred Hebrew and Aramaic texts of the previous two millennia. In a richly textured layering of literary and folkloristic motifs, An-sky presents a dramatic enactment of dybbuk possession to highlight the central issues of his age.

A child of a Hasidic family who as an adult was inspired by Haskalah, An-sky explores the confrontation between the "two worlds" of tradition and modernity, the shtetl and the secular world, physical reality and supernatural forces, hierarchic patriarchal society and Enlightenment individualism, rich and poor, sacred and profane and ultimately the boundaries between life and death, and this world and the world beyond.

In the historical evolution of Jewish ideas of afterlife, An-sky the secular socialist is the one who, inadvertently, brings mystically-based Lurianic teachings on *gilgul*, dybbuk and the postmortem survival of the soul to twentieth-century Yiddish theater, Polish film,[153] American television,[154] Broadway[155] and the contemporary world in general.[156]

The Dybbuk, or Between Two Worlds— *Synopsis of the Play*

The Dybbuk is a romantic drama of two star-crossed lovers, whose destiny to be together rejects the tradition of arranged marriages, and—like the tale of Romeo and Juliet—ends tragically in death.[157] It is a complex story filled with ancient kabbalistic teachings on the soul, visitations of spirits from the world beyond, trials and tribulations of dybbuk possession and technical details of an ancient exorcism ritual.

The Dybbuk is set in nineteenth-century Brinitz, Poland, a *shtetl* community in the Pale of the Settlement. As the play unfolds, we meet Khonon, a brilliant Talmud scholar and student of Kabbalah who is practicing arcane rituals from *Sefer Raziel*—a magical text on angels, amulets, names of God, protective spells, and the like.[158] Khonon also holds heretical Sabbatean ideas, claiming holiness can be found in sin and darkness.[159]

Next we meet a young woman named Leah, daughter of the wealthy Reb Sender. She and Khonon have a deep, clandestine yearning for one another, but this powerful romantic passion is aborted when Khonon discovers Leah is betrothed to another man. In shock and despair, realizing his ascetic practices and ablutions intended to woo Leah have failed, Khonon dies of a broken heart, and the play leads us to wonder if this is a consequence of his dabbling in perilous Sabbatean mystical lore.

Three months later, with Khonon dead and buried, Leah is about to be married to her betrothed groom, Menashe. On her wedding day, spirits from the beyond seem to take hold of her. Leah is encouraged by her father to visit her mother's grave in the cemetery to invite her mother to the wedding, as is the custom for brides and grooms to do. Leah also visits Khonon's grave and invites him to the wedding. But something untoward happens at the cemetery. Upon her return Leah begins acting fitfully and erratically, and as her groom places the bridal veil over her face, she rips the veil from her face and cries out in rage: "You are not my bridegroom!"[160] Leah faints and to everyone's shock it is discovered that a dybbuk has entered her body.

In Act III we meet a new character, a Hasidic master named Reb Azriel of Miropolye. Reb Sender brings Leah to see Reb Azriel who begins to question the dybbuk, realizing it is Khonon who claims Leah is his intended betrothed. Since Reb Azriel cannot convince the dybbuk to leave Leah's body, he prepares to convene an exorcism ritual, requesting the accoutrements of seven rams' horn, seven black candles, Torah scrolls from the Ark, and white robes for the participating minyan of men.[161]

Meanwhile the chief Rabbi of the town, Reb Shimshon, has had a dream in which Nissen, the deceased father of Khonon, reports that he and Leah's father, Reb Sender, had pledged to marry their children to one another. In this dream Nissen claims that his son Khonon died of a broken heart despondent that he did not get to marry his beloved Leah. With the death of Khonon, Nissen has no descendants to say Kaddish for him. *This little vignette of an unfulfilled material pledge is a crucial underpinning to this whole story.*

Reb Azriel and the local chief Rabbi, convene a rabbinical court to hear the claims of Nissen, Khonon's deceased father. Speaking on behalf of Nissen, Reb Azriel requests that the court hold Sender responsible for Khonon's death. The rabbinical court rules that Sender must donate half of his fortune to the poor and recite the mourner's Kaddish for Nissen and Khonon.

Following these pronouncements of the rabbinical court, wedding preparations are set to resume. But first the dybbuk must be exorcised. Leah is then brought before Reb Azriel, who orders the dybbuk to leave. But this dybbuk is not one to obey. So in full regalia—with fifteen men in white robes, with rams' horns, black candles, and Torah scrolls—Reb Azriel resumes the exorcism ritual, in a manner consistent with that described in kabbalistic texts.[162]

> Rise up, O Lord! Let your enemies fly from and be dispersed;[163] let them dissolve in the air like smoke. Sinful and rebellious spirit! With the power of Almighty God and with the authority of the holy Torah, I, Azriel the son of Hadas, sever all the threads that bind you to the world of the living and to the body and soul of the maiden Leah the daughter of Hannah.[164]

The ritual ends with the dybbuk seemingly vanished, and Reb Azriel prepares to lead the bride to the huppah, the bridal canopy. But the marriage is not to be, as Leah rejects marrying her chosen bridegroom, instead still cleaving to Khonon. In the culminating dramatic intensity Leah's voice is heard, from off in the distance: "I am enveloped in a blaze of light. My bridegroom, my destined one, I am united with you for all eternity. Together we will soar higher and higher, ever higher."[165] The stage goes dark, and Reb Azriel says, with a bowed head. "We are too late."[166] Leah has died to be reunited with her destined beloved in the afterlife realms where their souls are intertwined. And with this, the dramatic production ends.

Seeing *The Dybbuk* as a Jewish text on the afterlife, albeit in the literary form of a play, it is a goldmine of traditional teachings on the afterlife. Conversations between people, direct encounter with the dybbuk, and the bizarre and fascinating exorcism ritual all reveal a panorama of folk and philosophical images about postmortem spirits and the soul after death.

We shall now present sketches of various themes evidenced in *The Dybbuk*, demonstrating again how Yiddish literature transmitted Jewish afterlife philosophy in spite of the normative secular worldview of nineteenth- and twentieth-century Jewish thought.

The Thin Veil Between the Living and the Dead

Throughout *The Dybbuk* there is a perpetual awareness of the omnipresence of beings from the other side of the transition between life and death. This is not a world in which the dead are buried twenty exits north on the interstate highway and forgotten but one in which deceased loved ones continually dwell in close proximity to the living.

When we first meet Leah, she walks into the house of prayer in Brinitz accompanied by her elderly grandmother Frade. She has come to the synagogue to see old embroidered Torah Ark coverings. Why? Because she plans to embroider a new one to commemorate the Yahrzeit, anniversary, of her mother's death. And, says her grandmother Frade, "when the hanging is fixed in front of the Holy Ark, her mother's pious soul will rejoice in Paradise [Gan Eden]."[167] There is a sense here that the merit of benevolent activities done on behalf of one who has died impacts their soul in the world beyond in a beneficent way. This notion is articulated very explicitly in a unique, contemporary Hebrew text called *L'illui Neshamha: For the Elevation of the Soul*, which states:

> The essence of a woman's merit in the world to come [is based upon] her children serving God, doing God's will and being God-fearing. If her children are God-fearing in their hearts, and engage in Torah and *mitzvot*, after she is in her eternal resting-place [*beit olamah*] these deeds are all attributed to her as if she is alive and doing all the *mitzvot* herself, even as she is in the higher realms of the World to Come.[168]

This certainly stands in contrast to our Western secular notion that assumes dead is dead and there is no connection with the deceased other than through our memories.

Further: Grandma Frade explains to Leah that "the synagogue is always sad because the dead come to pray at midnight and leave their sorrows behind."[169] Frade's comment here is emblematic of the mindset of the old world shtetl, where it was believed that the dead would congregate overnight in the synagogue. According to Joshua Trachtenberg, author of *Jewish Magic and Superstition - A Study in Folk Religion*, a tradition evolved of knocking on a synagogue door before entry in the morning that served to notify spirit worshippers that the living were about to enter and it was time to depart.[170] The synagogue of An-sky's world is teeming with life—of the dead!

Stage directions of Act II are filled with intimations of spirits from the world beyond. In the square adjacent to the old synagogue in Brinitz is a solitary tombstone with the inscription: "Here lie the holy and pure bride and groom who were martyred for their faith in the year 5408"[171]—1648 CE—the year of the Chmielnicki massacres in Poland in which upwards of 100,000 Jews were brutally murdered by Cossack marauders.[172]

This is a theatrical representation of what An-sky discovered from his ethnographic research. Traveling in the villages of Volhynia he noticed memorial relics called *khosen-kale-kvorim* (groom and bride graves), and was told that at weddings guests would dance with the newly married couple seven times around such memorials.[173] The play tells of a young bride and groom who were slaughtered by the Chmielnicki brigands, as they were being led to the wedding canopy, and buried on the very spot where their lives were snuffed out. And as one of the characters says: "Each time the rabbi performs a wedding ceremony he hears sighs coming from the grave. In order to bring comfort and cheers to the buried bride and groom, it has long been a custom in our town to dance around the grave after every wedding."[174]

The *khosen-kale-kvorim* memorials became conduits to the realm of the deceased ancestors, and their memory honored and embodied through dance. The background to this representation of interconnection with deceased spirits in the world beyond is expressed through a particular ritual activity called the *toytntants*—the dance of death; in French, *danse macabre*. In the play, the scene unfolds in a bustling courtyard outside Reb Sender's home, where guests gather with joy to celebrate Leah's long-awaited wedding. As a wealthy man of the village, Reb Sender has invited "poor men and women, cripples, children and old people"[175] to share food, drink and partake in the festivities. As the bride-to-be begins to dance with a half-blind old woman, who keeps feverishly spinning her around, suddenly Leah enters a trance, gripped by otherworldly spirits:

> (*Eyes closed, head thrown back, speaks as if in a trance*) They held me, they surrounded me, they pressed themselves against me and pushed their cold, dry fingers into my flesh. My head was spinning, I grew faint. And then someone lifted me high into the air and carried me away—far, far away.[176]

In the 1937 Yiddish film version of *Der Dibuk*, this scene of dancing with death is superbly highlighted. With passion, the Angel of Death, wearing a white death mask, dances fervently with the entranced bride.[177] One of the most famous choreographic scenes of Yiddish cinema, this scene from the film conveys the presence of a roomful of spirits of the dead, including Khonon.

This custom of a *toytntants*—the dance of death—is said to date back to the time of the Black Death. At Christian and Jewish weddings, one of the guests would dress as death symbolizing the victory of life over disease and death.[178] To this day, in some Hasidic communities, a remnant of this custom, a *techies ha-meysim tants*, dance of revival of the dead, is done at weddings.[179] Through this image An-sky presents a community spectacle in which a window to the world beyond has opened and the living and the dead commingle.

Souls of the Dead, Afterlife and Reincarnation

Following the dance of death, the sense of the veil between worlds is highlighted in the discussion Leah and her grandmother Frade are having about invisible spirits and souls. Their conversation echoes the dialectic between folk beliefs that the dead are present in the human realm, and philosophical teachings that transcendent souls of the dead enter the heavenly Gan Eden. The content of their dialogue could easily have been between two Rabbis of the Zohar.

> "Grandma, we are not surrounded by evil spirits but by souls of people who have died before their time. It is they who watch every move we make and listen to everything we say,"[180] says Leah.
>
> "God help you child!" replies her grandmother. "What are you talking about? Souls? What souls? Pure, undefiled souls fly up to heaven and find eternal rest in Paradise [Gan Eden]."[181]

In continuing the conversation, we hear of Leah's yearning for her beloved Khonon. Her curiosity about the afterlife fate of Khonon's soul, sounds like both a philo-sophical oration and the lament of one deeply bereaved:

> No Grandma, they are here with us. (*In a different tone*) A person is born to live a long life. But if he dies before his time what happens to his unloved life, his joys and his sorrows, the ideas he did not have time to develop, the deeds he had no chance to do? What happens to the children who were to have been born to him? Where are they? Where? (*Thoughtfully*).[182]

Desperate to understand what happened to the con-sciousness and passion of Khonon's life, her words can be just as easily be spoken today by one who has lost a loved one suddenly:

> Once there was a young man with a lofty soul and a profound intelli-gence—a long life lay before him. And then in an instant, his life was cut down; strangers came to bury him in foreign soil. (*Sorrowfully*) What happened to his unlived life, his unspoken words, his unuttered prayers? Grandma, when the flame of a candle is snuffed out, you can relight it and it burns to the end. So how can the uncompleted life of a person be stamped out forever? How can it? . . .

No Grandma, a human life cannot be lost. When a person dies before his time his soul returns to complete the span of life which he was given on earth, to finish the life he began, to feel the joys and sorrows he did not live to know.[183]

Leah continues speaking about how souls of the dead continue to interact in the physical world. Consumed by acute grief she senses the reality of Khonon's presence in the world. These thoughts parallel teachings in rabbinic and kabbalistic literature, and folk stories of the *Ma'aseh Book* described earlier:

I will go to the cemetery today and ask [my mother] to lead me to the bridal canopy together with my father. And she will come; and afterwards she will dance with me. So it is with all souls who were taken from this world before their time. They are with us but we don't see them or feel their presence . . . (*Hushed*) Grandma, if one concentrates very hard, it is possible to see them and hear their voices and even know their thoughts.[184]

In response to Leah's questioning about the fate of one who died, the specific destiny of Khonon's soul, an enigmatic character of the play known as the Messenger, shows up here. His theatrical function is to weave together elements of the story, and offer words of wisdom. His message is drawn from *gilgul* teachings in Zohar and Lurianic Kabbalah, speaking of multiple incarnations and rebirth into animal bodies:[185]

> The souls of the dead do return to the world, but not as disembodied spirits. There are souls which must go through several incarnations before they are finally purified. (*Leah listens with close attention*) Sinful souls return to the earth in animals, in birds, in fish, and even at times in plants.[186]

Continuing, the Messenger articulates a point of view characteristic of Hasidism, that one can experience spiritual redemption through devotion to the Rebbe or tzaddik:[187] "They cannot achieve purification through their own efforts but must wait for a zaddik, a holy man, to free them and make them pure. And then there are souls who enter the body of a newborn child and purify themselves through their own deeds."[188] This comment serves to prepare the audience to meet Reb Azriel of Miropolye who will conduct a ritual to exorcise the dybbuk that has possessed Leah.

The Rebbe as Exorcist

At the start of Act III An-sky brings to the stage Reb Azriel of Miropolye. Although there were Hasidim from Miropolye, there is no known Hasidic Rebbe by that name. Reb Azriel represents an archetypal tzaddik who, like many of the Rebbes, was a psychopomp (from Greek *psychopompos*, "guide of souls"), able to commune with souls of the dead. Reb Azriel is said to be in a lineage of great Hasidic Rebbes: his grandfather, Reb Velvele, a renowned scholar, and disciple of the Baal Shem Tov "used to exorcize a dybbuk without using spells or incantations; he simply raised his voice and gave one piercing scream."[189]

Historically, Reb Azriel is representative of a long-standing tradition of kabbalistic Rabbis and Hasidic wonder-workers known to have done exorcisms.[190] Among the kabbalists, Joseph Karo, Hayyim Vital and his son, Samuel Vital; in Italy, Judah Ma-Tov; in Iraq, Sason ben Mordecai Shindookh; and Judah Petayah, active in the Baghdad into the 1930's; and among the Hasidim over a dozen Rebbes including the Maggid of Kozhnits; Shalom of Belz; Issacher Dov Baer of Radoshitz; and Rabbi Solomon of Bobov.[191]

In the play Sender requests of Reb Azriel to perform an exorcism ritual to banish the dybbuk. Continuing to be possessed by the spirit of the deceased Khonon, Leah is brought before Reb Azriel, screaming in the angry voice of the dybbuk. The exorcism is about to begin.

In his book, *Between Worlds: Dybbuks, Exorcists, and Early Modern Judaism*, J.H. Chajes describes how historical accounts of spirit possession always begin with extensive interviews to elicit background information from the possessing spirit.[192]

Reb Azriel commences his interrogation of the dybbuk: "Dybbuk, I command you to tell me who you are!" But the dybbuk is coy, not very forthcoming: "Rebbe of Miropolye, you know very well who I am, but I don't want to reveal my name in front of others." When pressed further about why he has possessed Leah, he replies: "Because I am her intended."[193] Here, in the first allusion to the cause of the possession, Khonon claims that he, not Menashe, is destined to marry Leah. While elements of this story parallel historical dybbuk narratives, unique here— after all, it is still fiction—is that Leah is possessed by a "jilted" lover, claiming that she is rightfully his. More often, the dybbuk does not necessarily know the person who is possessed, and in many cases, the possessed one has committed some kind of sin.[194]

Try as he will, Reb Azriel cannot convince the dybbuk to leave Leah's body: "Rebbe of Miropolye...you cannot impose your will on me. I have no place to go," says the dybbuk.[195] Again Reb Azriel commands the dybbuk to "leave the maiden's body [or] you will be excommunicated and given over to the angels of destruction."[196] Yet the dybbuk is reluctant and persistent: "In the name of the Almighty God I am enjoined to my intended forever and will never leave her."[197] Unsuccessful in expelling the dybbuk, Reb Azriel convenes a minyan of ten men and requests of them authority and permission to carry out an exorcism ritual.

Next we see specific elements used in a Jewish exorcism. Reb Azriel asks for seven rams' horns, seven black candles, and Torah scrolls from the Ark, as each of the men don white robes. This sombre scene accurately portrays exorcism rituals carried out in a synagogue or house of study by kabbalistic and Hasidic leaders. Participants forming the *minyan* would have prepared by fasting, bathing in a *mikve*, a ritual bath, and would be wearing a white *kitel*, the sacred garment one wears on Yom Kippur.[198]

Describing the phenomenology of such a ritual, Rachel Elior writes:

> Conducted in a sacred public space, the exorcism ceremony in the first instance embodies a confrontation with the world of the dead and a battle between holiness and impurity—a battle fraught with intense danger and entailing a mystical struggle involving holy names and unities, sounding of the rams' horn, use of Torah scrolls, fumigation and adjurations, curses and communication.[199]

At this point in the story, there is a pause in the attempt to banish the dybbuk. And as the play moves into Act III, we encounter yet another dimension of communication with otherworldly spirits.

Dreams from the World of the Dead

To excommunicate a Jewish soul, protocol demands one first solicit permission from the local chief rabbi. Before he can proceed further, Reb Azriel defers Hasidic charisma to local *halakhic* authority, inviting the local chief rabbi to be a co-participant in the ritual. Reb Shimshon arrives, gives consent for the excommunication ritual, and at the same time brings profound news to Reb Azriel, revealed to him in a dream:

> Rebbe, do you remember a young Hasid by the name of Nissen ben Rivke, a

student of Kabbalah who used to come
to Brinitz to visit you regularly about
twenty years ago?. . .[He] appeared
three times in my dreams last night and
demand that I summon Sender of Brinitz to a rabbinical court [*Beth Din*] in his
name . . . [He] said that Sender caused
him the most grievous harm . . . I have
heard that the young man who died and
entered the body of Sender's daughter
was Nissen's son. [These dreams] speak
of a certain promise which Sender made
to Nissen and never fulfilled."[200]

We see in this passage the pre-modern Jewish view, evidenced in the *Ma'aseh Book* and Sholem Aleichem's *Fiddler
on the Roof,* that one takes seriously dream visitations from
the dead. Here, Khonon's father, Nissen, has manifested
from the world of spirits, demanding that Leah's father,
Sender of Brinitz be brought to a trial before a rabbinical
court, a *beth din.* There is clearly some kind of unknown,
unfinished business from the invisible realm of spirits play-
ing itself out, revealed through Reb Shimshon's dream.
An unfilled promise is longer than a lifetime, and, as
Nissen claims, must be fulfilled or settled even after death.
As a consequence of the night visitation, before proceed-
ing with the exorcism, Reb Azriel must address the dream
communication received from Nissen, Khonon's father.

As it turns out, there is an ancient Jewish ritual known
as *Pitron Halomot*, "interpretation of dreams." It is based
upon a dream interpretation formula found in the Talmud
that is as follows:

If one has seen a dream and does not remember what he saw, let him stand before the priests. . . and say as follows: Master of the Universe, I am Yours and my dreams are Yours, I dreamed a dream and I do not know what it is. Whether I have dreamed of myself, whether my friends have dreamed of me or whether I have dreamed of others, if the dreams are good, strengthen them and reinforce them like the dreams of Joseph. And if the dreams require healing, heal them like the bitter waters of Mara by Moses our teacher, and like Miriam from her leprosy, and like Hezekiah from his illness, and like the bitter waters of Jericho by Elisha. And just as You transformed the curse of Balaam the wicked into a blessing, so transform all of my dreams for me for the best. (Berachot 55b)

In medieval Jewish liturgy the practice of dream interpretation was expanded into a complete communal ritual.[201] As Act IV opens, Reb Azriel has convened a rabbinic tribunal and recites the exact opening lines of the dream interpretation formula found in Jacob Emden's *Siddur Beit Yakov,* dating from the mid-eighteenth century: "I have seen a good dream, I have seen a good dream. I have seen a good dream."[202] The two rabbinical judges who complete the tribunal respond: "You have seen a good dream; good it is and good may it be!"[203]

The traditional dream ritual is actually much longer than what is presented here. Nonetheless, the dream communication from Nissen is taken seriously, and the play now segues to Reb Azriel sending a messenger to the cemetery summoning Nissen, from the realm of the dead, to appear before the rabbinic court.

At this point in the play, a potent and compelling after-life drama is unfolding. Two discarnate beings—Khonon, the possessing dybbuk, and his father Nissen, who has made his presence known through the realm of dreams—are both directly in communication with the world of the living. This is a world in which the window between this world and the world beyond is wide open, and the two realms are in interaction with each other.

The Exorcism Ritual Fails and The Dybbuk Lives On

In Act IV the encounter with the dybbuk proceeds. Invited before the rabbinical court, Nissen makes known his claim against Sender. Perceiving his presence, one member of the rabbinical court utters: "I hear a voice, but I don't hear any words;" says another: "I hear words, but I don't hear a voice;" then Reb Shimshon, who can communicate to the members of the rabbinical court the content of Nissen's grievance, says: "He is here."[204] We observe here that there are different senses engaged for perceiving the realm of the dead; for some it is auditory, for some visual; and Reb Shimshon and Reb Azriel have powers of communication with the spirit of the dead. Many spiritual leaders throughout time and history have had such powers.[205]

Reb Azriel orders the dybbuk to leave: "Dybbuk! In
the name of the chief rabbi who is here beside me, in the
name of the holy congregation of Jews, in the name of
the great Sanhedrin of Jerusalem, I, Azriel, son of Hadas,
order you for the last time to leave the body of the maid-
en."[206] But this dybbuk is not one to obey. Speaking as the
dybbuk Leah replies, "I will not leave!" With his cadre of
accompanying spiritual advisors, all dressed in full regalia
and carrying the necessary ritual implements, Reb Azriel
began performing an exceptionally dramatic exorcism
ritual consistent with that described in kabbalistic texts,
such as the sixteenth-century *Shoshan Yesod ha-Olam*, which
delineates specific guidelines for the adjuration of spirits.[207]

"Unyielding spirit!" declares Reb Azriel. "Since you
will not submit to our rule, I deliver you to the authority of
the higher spirits who will expel you by force." The ram's
horn is sounded, using traditional New Year's blasts—first
tekiah, then *shevraim*—but the dybbuk is ferociously resistant. As the drama increases, Reb Azriel delivers what is
the final blow to the defiant dybbuk:

> Rise up, O Lord! Let your enemies fly
> from and be dispersed;[208] let them dis-
> solve in the air like smoke. Sinful and
> rebellious spirit! With the power of
> Almighty God and with the authority
> of the holy Torah, I, Azriel the son of
> Hadas, sever all the threads that bind
> you to the world of the living and to the
> body and soul of the maiden Leah the
> daughter of Hannah."[209]

That fierce pronouncement works; Leah desperately screams: "I'm lost!. . .I have no more strength to resist." And the ram's horns blast sounds one final time. "Do you swear to leave the body of the maiden Leah the daughter of Hannah, and promise never to return?" asks Reb Azriel. "I promise," says the dybbuk.

The ritual has come to an end, the black candles are extinguished, the black curtain removed from the Holy Ark, and the fourteen men take off their robes and depart. It appears that the dybbuk has vanished, so next Reb Azriel prepares to lead the bride to the *huppah*, the bridal canopy.

But the story of the dybbuk is not over yet. Following the ritual, Leah is dreamy, falling asleep. In an instant something strange happens to her; the dybbuk has returned. Khonon and Leah are like two lovers in dialogue with each other. Says Leah: "My heart was drawn to a bright star. In the deep of the night I shed sweet tears, and someone always appeared in my dreams." Khonon declares "I left your body in order to enter your soul." Leah's yearning escalates: "Return to me, my bridegroom, my husband. I will carry you in my heart, and in the still of the night you will come to me in my dreams and together we will rock our unborn babies to sleep."[210]

As An-sky's play moves towards a crescendo, wedding music is heard in the background. And we hear Leah cry out in desperation: "They are about to lead me to the wedding canopy to marry a stranger. Come to me, my bridegroom." The passionate longing Leah and Khonon have for each other is totally unleashed. "Come to me!" cries Khonon. "I am coming to you,"[211] Leah responds.

Nothing in life or death can stop the destiny the beloved maiden and desperate dybbuk have for one another.

In the culminating pinnacle of dramatic intensity Leah's voice is heard, seemingly from a distance: "I am enveloped in a blaze of light. My bridegroom, my destined one, I am united with you for all eternity. Together we will soar higher and higher, ever higher." The stage goes dark, and Reb Azriel says, with a bowed head. "We are too late."[212]

From the Messenger we hear the words one pronounces upon hearing the news of a death: "Blessed is the true Judge." Leah has died to be reunited with her destined beloved in the afterlife where their souls are intertwined.

This dybbuk story does not have a happy ending. It is a grievous tale of love and death, of two souls destined to be together, in a fateful reunion. An-sky makes a statement about the breakdown of traditional Jewish marriage practices in the age of modernity. And by weaving together Jewish teachings on the soul, afterlife, reincarnation, and the dybbuk in an innovative theatrical production, An-sky has bequeathed to Jewish life a creative masterpiece of heart, mind, and spirit that has had ongoing resurrections, not in the world beyond, but in this world. *The Dybbuk, or Between Two Worlds* keeps alive the slowly disappearing Jewish tradition of life after death in the early decades of the twentieth century, and to this day.

7

Images of Afterlife in the Writings of Isaac Bashevis Singer (1904-1991)

Biographical Background

Isaac Bashevis Singer was born into an Orthodox rabbinical family in Radzymin, Poland, in 1904. His father and both grandfathers were rabbis, his family roots connected to a long-standing Hasidic lineage. The men of the Singer family had been rabbis at least seven generations, and one of his ancestors was a disciple of the Baal Shem Tov.

In his youth, Singer received a traditional Jewish education, attending a rabbinical seminary in Warsaw where he also learned modern Hebrew and secular subjects. Within his own family, he was exposed to the opposing intellectual forces of his time. His father, Pinchas, who only spoke Yiddish, was a mystically inclined traditionalist deeply immersed in kabbalistic study and prayer. And his mother, Betsheva (in whose honor he took the middle name Bashevis), "was the quintessential rationalist, who defended her belief in God the Creator through reason argument but otherwise remained skeptical and pragmatic."[213] Singer's youth straddled the polarities of his parents' conflicted marriage, at first, living the old-world way of life on Krochmalna Street in Warsaw, and later immersed in Kabbalah while in his grandfather's village of Bilgoraj for three years during his adolescence, and also influenced by his older brother's secular Yiddish writing. These formative experiences left their impact on Singer's artistic and moral development. Singer had an active, versatile career as a journalist, critic, and writer of Yiddish short stories and novels. The early years of his literary life were spent in Warsaw, and in 1935, sensing the ominous threat of Hitler's rise to power, he migrated to New York and spent decades writing for the *Jewish Daily Forward*.[214]

Steeped in an understanding of Jewish tradition and the nuances of Jewish mysticism and supernatural folk traditions, for the remaining years of his life, Singer would compose fiction and memoirs about the world he had left behind in Poland. His writings mythologized nineteenth-century Polish Jewish life, chronicled the struggles between traditionalism and the world of modernity outside the shtetl, and, in his later years, captured the struggle Jewish immigrants from Eastern Europe went through in pursuing the ever-unattainable American dream. Singer wrote in Yiddish, and, after arriving in America, he always used the same typewriter his brother Joshua had given him as a gift.

Prolific for over fifty years, he published at least eighteen novels, more than a dozen collections of short stories, as well as children's books and memoirs.[215] Recognizing the universal significance of his literary work, he was awarded the Nobel Prize in Literature in 1978, becoming the first and only Yiddish writer to receive that honor.

Towards the end of his life Singer moved to Miami Beach, Florida, where he died on July 24th, 1991, at the age of 87 years old. He was buried in Emerson, New Jersey.

Isaac Bashevis Singer's Writings on the Afterlife

A spirit of mysticism and themes of death and afterlife permeate all of Isaac Bashevis Singer's writings. He grew up in a home in which there were frequent conversations about dead spirits possessing the living, souls reincarnated into animal bodies, and the constant threat of haunting goblins and demons.[216] In addition to being exposed to Kabbalah, as a young man Singer studied psychical research, the theosophy of Madame Blavatsky, and the anthroposophy of Rudolph Steiner, all of which had been quite popular in intellectual circles of the late-nineteenth century.[217] As a result Singer's writings utilize Jewish legend and superstition to tell stories of dybbuks, seances, psychics, conversations with the dead, and voices from the world beyond. At the same time, influenced by modernity, Singer's writings endeavor to bridge the conflicting forces of Enlightenment rationalism and traditional Jewish life, His characters are saints and scoundrels, seekers and skeptics, Hasidim and irreligious cynics, all in their own ways wrestling with issues of meaning, connection to the divine, and the reality of human mortality.[218]

Images of death and the afterlife based on rabbinic and kabbalistic teachings permeate Singer's fiction more than in any other author discussed in this book. One could fill an entire book with afterlife motifs in the works of Isaac Bashevis Singer. By way of example: in *The Magician of Lublin*, one of his characters states: "Only the body dies. The soul lives on. The body is like a garment. When a garment becomes soiled or threadbare, it is cast aside."[219] In *The Family Moskat* another character has a conversation with his dead wife, asking: "Hadassah, where are you now? Do you know? Do you exist? Was it possible that past time had no being? Was there nothing but the momentary present?"[220] In the story "Joy," there is a postmortem visitation; similarly in "Gimpel the Fool" a women appears in a dream, dressed in a shroud. In *Satan and Goray,* "The Dead Fiddler" and at least three other short stories tell of an unsuspecting character possessed by a dybbuk.[221] And in "Reaches of Heaven" both saints and sinners have to return to earth to make up for sins or omissions from previous lives.[222] Whether it is the doctrine of *gilgul,* images of Gehenna and Gan Eden, or postmortem wanderings of lost souls, Singer has them all, far more than we can explore here.

To shed light on the nuances of Singer's exploration of afterlife themes, we shall consider three of his works: 1) *Satan in Goray* (1933), his first novel, cast in the era of the renegade false Messiah Shabbatai Tzvi, which tells the tale of a possessing dybbuk; 2) "Sabbath in Gehenna"(1972), which as we shall see, is a short story which creatively weaves together traditional Jewish eschatology and modernist thought, and, 3) *Shadows on the Hudson*, (1957) one of his last novels, cast in New York City with Holocaust survivors facing the realities of meaning in the face of death and suffering.

Satan in Goray—
*A Historical Novel of Sabbateanism
and Dybbuk Possession*

Singer's very first novel, *Satan in Goray*, was written in Yiddish in 1933 and published in English translation in

1955. It is set in the Eastern European village of Goray, a traumatized community in the years immediately following the 1648 Chmielnicki massacres.

In the shadow of tragedy are men and women who have lost loved ones. Describing the aftermath of the destruction, Singer writes, "Corpses lay neglected in every street, with no one to bury them. Savage dogs tugged on dismembered limbs, and vultures and crows fed on human flesh."[223] Against this background we meet a cast of characters striving to rebuild their lives: the old town Rabbi, Benish Ashkenazi, who is working to restore Goray to its past glory, but, broken by the massacres, is too old and tired to do so; the formerly richest man in town, Reb Eleazar Babad; his sensual but disabled and epileptic daughter Rechele; and itinerant preachers Reb Itche Mates and Reb Gedaliya who bring to Goray the teachings of the self-proclaimed Messiah Shabbatai Tzvi, ushering in a whirlwind of chaotic hedonism rife with lust and the brazen transgression of every precept of Jewish law.[224]

As a historical novel capturing the spirit of seventeenth-century Jewish life, Singer invites readers to imagine and re-experience the chaos and confusion of Jewish community life amid the hope and anticipation of the long-awaited redemption from exile.[225] *Satan in Goray* describes the mass hysteria and messianic frenzy that grips Goray as the yearning for redemption spreads into every home and family.

The apostasy of Shabbatai Tzvi to Islam, which took place in 1666, was interpreted as a sign that the final days were about to arrive, and the accompanying belief was that on the way to salvation all evil had to be embraced.

Followers of Shabbatai Tzvi encourage residents to engage in sensual pleasures of sex, food and dancing, and as a consequence, an orgiastic spirit grips the village of Goray.

Central to the storyline of *Satan in Goray* is Rechele, the somewhat peculiar daughter of Reb Eleazar Babad. For a time, she is married to Reb Itche Mates and then, as the Sabbatean chaos sets in, Reb Gedalia sends Reb Itche Mates on a missionary journey, and seduces Rechele from her husband.

At first Rechele begins to prophesy and was revered as a holy woman. But as the anticipated messianic redemption of Shabbatai Tzvi does not materialize, Goray descends into chaos, orgiastic rituals, and every type of abomination. Finally, Rechele herself is defiled and possessed by a dybbuk, none other than Satan.[226] Amid a community filled with quarreling and division, the closing chapters of Singer's novel describe both dybbuk possession and exorcism,[227] similar to what appears in the *Ma'aseh Book* and in An-sky's *Dybbuk*.

Written in 1935, as the ascent of Nazism was on the horizon, *Satan in Goray* is a Jewish tale of spirits and dybbuks, and at the same time an allegorical warning of the dangers inherent in mass hysteria and surrender of cultural boundaries and parameters that define community life.

Afterlife Motifs in Satan in Goray

Embedded within Singer's *Satan in Goray* are various elements of Jewish beliefs about the afterlife, revealing the extent to which residents of Goray lived in a multi-dimensional world populated with spirits and ghosts. We are told about the early years of Rechele's life. Orphaned at the age of five, she was raised by a widower uncle, Reb Zeydel Ber, and his mother-in-law, a nasty and abusive stepmother who Rechele called Granny: "A woman nearly ninety, deaf, with a waxen, shriveled face, full of moles and clumps of yellowish hair."[228] Since Rechele tended to wander off from her home, to prevent her from doing so, Granny "persuaded Rechele that there were graves in the yard when ghosts flew about ceaselessly, seeking bodies to enter."[229]

When Rechele was twelve years old, the old woman died the morning before Yom Kippur. As she lay dying, her son-in-law Reb Zeydel Ber came into her room to check on the old woman, and "drawing a goose feather from his breast, he would hold it near the dying woman's nostrils to see whether she was still breathing."[230] Interestingly, in the sixteenth-century *Shulkhan Arukh*, Code of Jewish Law, it states: "After the departure of the soul, a light feather is placed at his nostrils. If it does not move, it clearly indicates he is dead."[231] This was the method of choice for determining if a person had died, and as the text indicates, death was not simply cessation of life but rather the departure of the soul. And in the world of Goray, there were a lot of souls of the deceased around.

Alone on Yom Kippur eve, in the synagogue of the village of Goray that had been ravaged not long ago by Chmielnicki's hooligans, "it was common knowledge that on this, the holiest of nights, when the awesome prayer of Kol Nidre was chanted, the air was full of those ghosts that would find no resting place in the Hereafter."[232] And more, "Rechele and her friends had once seen with their own eyes such a ghost pass by the candle and disappear in the hearth."[233] Alone in her house that evening, but a few hours after the corpse of her stepmother had been removed, Rechele heard low muttering sounds. "The sound seemed to come from beneath the earth, and it appeared to Rechele that it was the chanting of Kol Nidre. But then it dawned on her that it was the dead who were chanting."[234] As Rechele fell asleep that night, the thin veil between this world and the world beyond opened for her, and "in her dreams Granny came to her—her clothes in tatters, disheveled and haggard. The kerchief about her head was soaked with blood. 'Rechele! Rechele!' she screamed and rubbed the girl's face with a straw whisk." Once again we see how the dead appear in dreams, and in this case, it was not safe for Rechele to be in touch with the world of the dead.

Elsewhere in *Satan in Goray* the traditional rabbinic notion of resurrection of the dead is interwoven with Eastern European folk traditions. In Elul, the Hebrew month before *Rosh HaShana*, the Jewish New Year, it is customary to visit the cemetery, as if to symbolically give an end-of-year review to deceased loved ones, and invite them to be with us for the coming year. Known as *Kever Avot*, literally "the graves of the fathers," this is still practiced to this day, usually on the Sunday between *Rosh HaShanah*, and Yom Kippur.[235]

Singer writes how, amid the Sabbatean messianic fervor in Goray, each morning during the month of Elul,

> . . . crowds of women descended to the
> cemetery to bid the dead farewell; the

dead would not reach the holy land as soon as the living; when the Messiah came they would pass to the Land of Israel by way of the underground caverns.

For days the women lay prostrate on the graves, screaming and wailing, begging for forgiveness of the dead for deserting them, explaining that the day of resurrection was near, calling upon them to intercede for the living and kin and neighbors in the Hereafter. The wealthy cut wicks the length of the graves of their beloved to make candles for the study house.[236]

This passage is filled with a dynamic relationship between the world of the living and the realm of disembodied spirits. Entranced by the Sabbatean vision of messianic fulfillment, the people of Goray believed they would soon depart for the Holy Land (this theme is written about extensively in this novel). Given how the living and dead are deeply interconnected, in advance of their anticipated departure, townsfolk feel the need to say goodbye to the deceased, asking them to act as intercessors on behalf of the living.

Further, the passage speaks of how the people from Goray will get to the Holy Land before the dead; only at the time of the resurrection will the buried dead make their way to Jerusalem through underground passageways. This idea is based on a rabbinic teaching that at the end of time, "God will make underground passages for the righteous who, rolling through them like skin bottles will get to the Land of Israel" (Pesikta Rabbati 1:6). We see how skillfully Singer weaves traditional teachings into his story. Even more, at the end of the earlier quoted paragraph is a rather cryptic passage about how the "wealthy cut wicks the length of the graves of their beloved to make candles for the study house." Wicks the length of graves for candles? What is that all about?

As the feminist scholar Chava Weissler has noted, there was a tradition of women making candles for Yom Kippur. On the eve Yom Kippur women would go to the cemetery, measure the length of a grave using a candlewick, and afterwards "[rub] the wicks with wax, reciting prayers over them. Each woman made two candles, a larger and thicker one for the souls of the living. . .and a smaller thinner one for the souls of the dead."[237] Singer interweaves this folk practice in with rabbinic teachings on resurrection, all the while writing about dybbuks, spirits, and the world beyond, revealing a rich tapestry of afterlife imagery.

Meeting the Dybbuk of Goray

After An-sky's *The Dybbuk*, *Satan in Goray* is the second best-known possession story in all of Yiddish literature. In the last two chapters of the novel we read descriptions of the dybbuk attaching itself to Rechele, and the formalized ritual practice to expel that dybbuk. The phenomenological descriptions of dybbuk possession and exorcism portrayed by Singer correspond with historical dybbuk narratives in the literature of Lurianic Safed.[238]

Amid the Sabbatian frenzy in Goray, Rechele is gripped by states of transcendental inspiration: in her nighttime visions angels, prophets, and ancient Rabbis would visit with her, and

> . . . calling by name angels and sera-
> phim, she told of the heavenly mansions
> and the lords ruling in each of them; the
> cryptic passages in the Book of Daniel
> so baffling to ordinary minds were
> explained by her—it was clear to all that
> the spirit of prophecy had entered into
> Rechele.[239]

But over time, as word of Shabbatai Tzvi's apostasy spread, residents of Goray were left emotionally and spiritually devastated, a devouring famine spread through the town, and for Rechele "the holy angels ceased appearing before her."[240] "Piety and the grace of God left," and in its place, her inner life was filled with darkness and fear. Sinking lower and darker, Rechele was suddenly possessed and violated by Satan, who visited and would torment her at night. Even the local peasants "also knew that Satan had entered the body of a daughter of the Jews."[241]

Possessed by a dybbuk, as Rechele spoke, the voice that came from her was no longer her own; in its place, the dybbuk wailed in a terrorizing voice of a man, first condemning Rechele's husband Reb Gadalyia, and then—as dybbuks do—confessing his own sins:

> How then shall I not cry and how
> then shall I not wail: Seeing that
> when I walked among the living I pol-
> luted my soul and transgressed every

transgression cited in the Torah . . . On
the holy Sabbath day I did work and I
did eat of the pig and other forbidden
foods. And on Yom Kippur I made a
feast for spite and drank wine and gave
myself to unbridled desire and I also lay
with beasts, animals and fowls.[242]

A deceased, discarnate being not able to move into the
realm of purgation of Gehenna to be purified and purged
of defilements, nor able pass to another incarnation, the
dybbuk describes his own death and what happens immediately afterwards:

And when they had laid me in the grave
and piled the last shovelful of earth
upon me there came to me the Angel
Dumah: And he rapped on my grave
with his fiery rod and the grave split
open at once: And he called *Mah Sheme-
cha* (What is thy name?) and I could not
remember for I had not prayed; And
the angel cried Thou foul seed Thou
sinner against the Lord of Israel. Tarry
not here and abandon this grave and
fly away to the hollow of the sling [*kaf-ha-
kela*] . . .And I tried to implore him but
he tore the shrouds from my body and
he beat me with his fiery rods and he
drove me out.[243]

In a rich literary style, Singer once again weaves traditional images of the afterlife journey into his fiction. In rabbinic literature, the Angel of Death is known as Dumah (Midrash Ps.11:6) and in kabbalistic legend, a dying person is asked their name by the escorting Angel of Death as a way to awaken them from postmortem somnambulance into a consciousness of their deeper self.[244] Similarly, the image of the dybbuk sent to "the hollow of the sling" is a kabbalistic metaphor referring to *kaf ha-kela*, the catapult, or what Schachter-Shalomi calls "a cosmic centrifuge" that helps the soul eliminate residual psychic impurities.[245] And finally, the dybbuk being beaten with fiery rods is an image taken from medieval midrash; in the text *Rabbi Joshua ben Levi and the Seven Compartments of Gehinnom*, "an angel stands with a rod of fire"[246] Singer is clearly fully aware of the mythic metaphors embedded in Jewish afterlife traditions and conveys them in strikingly explicit ways throughout the novel.

Exorcising the Dybbuk

Outrageous behavior of the dybbuk continued unabated, so Reb Mordecai Joseph, known for his work in redeeming souls, had Rechele brought to the synagogue that he might drive out the evil spirit. But the dybbuk continued to rage and blaspheme; it desecrated God's name and shouted obscenities, shamed men and women of the town by revealing secret sins of each one, put the "wives of respectable men to shame and revealed that the rabbi's wife had played the whore."[247]

Reb Mordecai Joseph began interrogating the dybbuk to discover how he was able to enter Rechele and gain control over her. The dybbuk reported that "the woman desired to start a fire with two flint stones and the spark would not light the wick: And she cried out the name of Satan: And the moment I heard this I entered her body."[248] It is often some transgression committed by the one who is possessed that opens a gateway for the dybbuk.

Next Reb Mordecai Joseph begins preparing for the ritual, gathering traditional exorcism implements—a censer, onycha, wax, incense, other spices, and glowing coals. He ordered black candles to be lit and covered himself in a white robe as a minyan of ten men donned prayer shawls and phylacteries, with one man designated to sound the ram's horn. After the doors of the Holy Ark were opened and a Torah scroll removed, the Rebbe-exorcist declared, "Be quick and fly. Or I shall excommunicate thee and drive thee off by force."[249]

Rechele, still in the grasp of the dybbuk, was writhing and sputtering uncontrollably and as the ram's horn was sounded, Reb Mordecai Joseph declared: "I excommunicate thee: May every curse and every ban . . . fall on thy head if thou forsake not the body of this woman immediately and out of hand."[250]

At first the dybbuk seemed to comply with the edict to leave, crying out to Reb Mordecai, "Make me free of the ban and I undertake to leave in good faith for I can withstand the sacred no longer."[251] In response Reb Mordecai Joseph agreed to lift the ban against the dybbuk and promised to study Mishna and recite the Mourner's Prayer on behalf of his soul.

In the writings of Isaac Luria we find a rationale delineating the importance of reciting Kaddish on behalf of the deceased's soul:

> As to the Kaddish which is recited
> during the first year . . . the reason is not
> as is commonly believed by the general
> population that it only helps to save the
> soul of the departed from the judgment
> of purgatory. There is another benefit
> (advantage), the Kaddish leads the soul
> into the Garden of Eden ("paradise")
> and it helps to raise the soul from level
> to level. (Isaac Luria, *Shaar HaKavanot*,
> Kaddish).[252]

But this dybbuk was wily and deceitful and reneged on the agreement to leave Rechele saying "No, Here it is better for me and I shall not depart."[253] A fierce battle of wills ensued for many hours until all the ritual declarations, the blowing of the ram's horn, and the adjurations to drive out the dybbuk prevailed. Finally, in a flash of fire, the dybbuk departed.

And while the story seems to be heading towards a happy ending, the tale of this dybbuk, perhaps patterned on An-sky's play, likewise does not end well. After days of restlessness following the expulsion of the dybbuk, "when the women came to Rechele to tend to her they found her dead and her body was already cold."[254] As she was being buried, a Kaddish was said over her grave. And *Satan in Goray* ends with this declaration:

> Let none attempt to force the Lord: To
> end pain within the world: The Mes-
> siah will come in God's own time: And
> free men of despair and crime: Then
> death will put his sword: And Satan die

abjured, abhorred: Lillith will vanish
the night: The exile will end and all be
light: Amen Selah.[255]

Isaac Bashevis Singer's *Satan in Goray* fulfills a number
of different functions. First of all, this novel is intended as a
morality tale, as dybbuk stories often were. Set historically
in the era of Shabbatai Tzvi, Singer tells this tale to warn
of the excesses of blind obedience to the messianic ideal-
ism and moral licentiousness that plagues the residents of
Goray. But more than this, as a novel written in Poland in
the 1930, this novel is at the same time a warning against
the impending authoritarian fascism of its time. And in
some ways, perhaps it is as relevant today as it was when
first written.

And finally, as we have demonstrated, this novel brings
to the fore Jewish ideas of life after death to a world of
twentieth-century modernity in which ideas of the afterlife are slowly disappearing from communal philosophical
discourse. Singer's writing are a midrashic modality of
the twentieth century, serving as both a repository and a
transmitter of Jewish conceptions of life after death.

"Sabbath in Gehenna"—
Political Discourse and Jewish Eschatology

The short story "Sabbath in Gehenna," originally
written in Yiddish under the title *Shabes in Gehenem* was published in 1972, and is thus the most contemporary of the
literature examined thus far in this book.[256] The English

version, translated by Singer himself, was included in the 1974 anthology, *The Death of Methuselah and Other Stories.*[257]

This humorous and thought-provoking short story epitomizes a syncretistic blending of rabbinic eschatology with Jewish political thought of the late nineteenth and early twentieth century. Detailing the conversations sinners in Gehenna are having, "Sabbath in Gehenna" presents a panorama of voices of modern Jewish life peppered with traditional midrashic motifs, echoing centuries of ancient Jewish texts.

"On the Sabbath, as is known, the fires do not burn in Gehenna"[258] — so begins the story, and immediately here Singer is drawing from rabbinic (Pesikta Rabbati 23:8) and kabbalistic sources describing how on "Sabbath, New Moons, special occasions and festivals the fire is extinguished there [in Gehenna], and they [sinners] have a respite from punishment" (Zohar, II, 151a).

Continuing, Singer specifies what Sabbath is like in Gehenna with cessation from punishment in effect:

> The beds of nails are covered with sheets. The hooks on which the wicked males and females hang—by their tongues for gossip, their hands for theft, their breasts for lechery, their feet for running after sin—are concealed behind screens. The piles of red-hot coals and icy snow onto which transgressors are flung are invisible that day. The angels of destruction have put away their fiery rods.[259]

This is essentially a paraphrasing of *Masekhet Gehin-nom*—*Tractate Of Gehinnom*, the medieval legendary text in which Rabbi Joshua ben Levi is given a narrated tour of Gehenna by Prophet Elijah:

> He showed me men hanging by their hair; and he said to me, "These were the men . . . hanging by their tongues; these were they that had slandered. Others were hanging by their hands, these were they that had stolen and robbed . . . Others were hanging by their feet; these were they that had run to sin. He showed me women hanging by their breasts; these were they that uncovered their breasts before men, to make them sin . . . He showed me further men that were fed on fiery coals; these were they who had blasphemed.[260]

With this as a backdrop, Singer then sets up the fundamental thematic core of this story: "The freethinkers (there are many of them in Gehenna) sit on logs and converse. As is usually the case with enlightened ones, their topic is *how to improve their lot, how to make a better Gehenna* [emphasis mine]."[261] Against the background of hundreds and hundreds of texts on the afterlife, evidenced on over three millennia of Jewish history and thought,[262] this one is the funniest and most curious text of all—sinners are discussing how to make Gehenna a better place! This is the marriage of Jewish afterlife myth and socialist, or Bundist, political thought. The General Union of Jewish

Workers in Lithuania, Poland and Russia, known by its Yiddish name, the Bund, was a secular Jewish socialist movement in the early twentieth century which had as it primary goal to improve social conditions of the masses of Jewish workers in Eastern Europe.[263] Many of the Yiddishists like Sholem Aleichem, I.L. Peretz, S. An-sky, and obviously Isaac Bashevis Singer were intellectually aligned with the program of the Bund. Singer artfully works this political ideology into his storyline, and the rest of the story uses the backdrop of Gehenna to depict a dance of characters representing variations of the Yiddish socialist political spectrum.

The conversation begins with one sinner, Yankel Farseer (interesting name!) articulating a list of demands to be presented to the angel Dumah: that a week in Gehenna be reduced to four days, that all sinners be granted a six-week vacation with permission to "return to earth and break the Ten Commandments without being punished, [and further], that we should not kept away from our beloved sisters, the female sinners. We demand sex and free love."[264]

Less work, vacation time, and more sex—seems to be a reasonable request; but not everyone was in agreement. Another more radical sinner replied, with cynicism: "The angel Dumah is not afraid of your demands and petitions." Representing the revolutionary spirit of the era and advocating armed struggle, he declared: "We must arm ourselves. Rub out the angel Dumah, storm the court of heaven, break a few ribs among the righteous . . . take over paradise [Gan Eden] . . ."[265]

Yet another sinner, "a petit bourgeois who had fallen into hell for swindling," cried out in opposition, "Where will you get arms in hell? They don't give us a single knife or fork." Echoing traditional rabbinic teachings that the punishment of the wicked in Gehenna is time-limited, lasting a maximum of twelve months,[266] the sinner went on: "Besides, Gehenna does not last longer than a year . . . I am supposed to end my term on the day after Purim. If we begin the conspiracy now, the term may be prolonged."[267] It was clear there was no emerging agreement as to goals or tactics.

Reflecting the spirit of intellectualism characteristic of the Yiddishist Haskalah, another resident, "a sinner with eyeglasses," proposed that "we should concentrate mainly on culture. Before we come with maximal demands like six-week vacations with sex and free love, we must show the angels that we are *sinners* with spiritual goals." Sinners with spiritual goals! What a radical image Singer puts forth here. Never before has there been such a notion in the three-thousand-year history of Jewish eschatology.

Outlining his vision, which mirrors exactly what took place in the Jewish communities of Warsaw and the Lower East Side, this sinner proposed "that we publish a magazine . . . and its name should be *The Gehennanik*:"

> When you sign a petition, the angels take one look at it and they throw it away . . . a magazine they would read. The righteous in paradise [Gan Eden] expire from boredom. They are overfed with the secrets of Torah. They want to know what's going on in hell. They are curious about our view of the world, our way of thinking, our sex fantasies,

and, most of all, they are intrigued by
the fact that we are still atheists. A series
of articles, "The Atheists in Gehenna,"
would become a smash hit in paradise
[Gan Eden].[268]

The Yiddishist movement, in both nineteenth-century Europe and early twentieth-century America, was diverse and multi-pronged, bridging political, social, literary, and cultural perspectives. Putting forth another viewpoint characteristic of early modern Yiddishist culture, a young-looking sinner, with shoulder-length hair offered yet an additional suggestion:

Why publish a magazine? Why not open
a theater? We have a shortage of paper
here. Besides, its so hot that the magazine will catch fire . . . My advice is that
we should organize a theatrical group
. . . We will perform on Sabbaths and
all holidays . . . Theater is the best form
of propaganda. It may very well be that
the saints and the angels will visit our
theater to see our plays. And between
one act and the other, we would explain
to them our point of view, our situation
and our philosophy.[269]

Amidst the obvious lack of consensus among the sinners of Gehenna, there was still one more voice to be heard, a sinner, who had been a politician during his lifetime. He said:

Culture will not solve our problem, and neither will the theater. What we really need is a progressive political party built on democratic principles . . . I have heard from a very reliable source that there is a liberal group among the angels who are asking for reforms in Gehenna.[270]

They want us to have a five-day week. Besides Saturdays and holidays, we should be given a vacation in the World of Illusions.[271] Some of them would request that the nails on the beds of nails should be two millimeters shorter. I was told that there is some change in their attitude toward homosexuality, lesbianism and certainly masturbation.[272]

Singer is slowly moving in for the story's denouement, as the politician continues: "We could do a lot, but we need money."[273] Everyone is astounded but he goes on, quoting Ecclesiastes 10:19: "And money answereth all things." With money there is so much that can be accomplished without revolution; there will be no need for petitions, newspapers, theater, culture. The politician continued, wanting to enlighten his listeners on all that could be accomplished in Gehenna with money, but then something quite decisive took place: "At that instant the Sabbath ended." The Shabbat afternoon discourse of improving conditions in Gehenna instantly faded. Suddenly, the cast of characters was gone; even the politician claiming that money was the magical solution to all did not endure. And the moment Sabbath came to an end, "The fires [of Gehenna] leaped up again. The nails on the beds began to glow with heat. The punishing demons grabbed up their rods, and a lashing and a whipping and a hanging and a wailing erupted once more."[274] It all faded as if in a dream, and the torments of Gehenna resumed—end of story.

Envisioning Gehenna with a creative, imaginary spin, in "Sabbath in Gehenna" Singer gives voice to the diverse ideologies of modern Yiddishist life—grassroots organizing, violent revolution, newspaper writing, theater, culture, and politicians seduced by money. But in the final analysis none of these perspectives endures, and the fires of Gehenna are reignited. Perhaps the message here is the same one that underlie rabbinic afterlife teachings on Gehenna. Even with the changing hues of time, history and culture, each individual is called upon to live a life that is moral, ethical and imbued with a sense of the holy; and to the extent that we fail to do so in our lifetime, at the end of life each person is called to live with the consequence of their activities of embodied life.

Shadows on the Hudson—
Holocaust Survivors Searching for Meaning

Shadows on the Hudson, one of Singer's last novels, is set in New York in 1948, in the shadow of the Holocaust. Originally serialized in 1957, appearing twice weekly in the Yiddish newspaper, *The Jewish Daily Forward*, a post-humous English translation of this book was published in 1998.[275] It is a story of prosperous Holocaust refugees rebuilding their lives in America after World War II. Yet, as relatively recent work, written in an entirely different era than much of the Yiddish literature examined thus far, it presents a modern narrative grappling with a modern dilemma—the search for meaning in the aftermath of the Holocaust.

We meet the book's main protagonists at an Upper West Side dinner party; they are a group of characters who are archetypal representations of the intellectual and spiritual worldview of Jewish life in postwar America. The host, Boris Makaver, is a wealthy, pious businessman who stands for capitalism; his other guests include a devoted communist, a spiritualist who dabbles in seances, an intellectual, a cynic, a hedonist, and even a person who is chronically indecisive. Echoing the multivocal literary style of "Sabbath in Gehenna," in this novel Singer gives voice to the array of divergent responses to the underbelly of despair in the aftermath of the Nazi genocide. (Singer never uses the term "Holocaust," only after the Eichmann trial in 1961 did that term emerge specially to define the events of World War II).[276]

In *Shadows on the Hudson*, Singer speaks "in an unfamiliar raw and brutal voice, the grandfatherly Yiddish writer stripped of the kindly, gentle tone and the flights of supernatural fantasy that we mostly know him by."[277] It is a tale of love and lust; promiscuous sex and extramarital affairs; the soulless nature of New York; traumatized characters philosophizing on Kabbalah, Spinoza, Nietzsche and even more; and—for our discussion here— lots of talk on death, afterlife, and the fate of souls killed in the Holocaust.

Shadows on the Hudson is an unwieldy novel, Singer's largest at 550 pages in length. Rather than tell the story, here we shall present a collage of images and themes, showing how Singer uses traditional Jewish afterlife motifs, and chronicles wrestling with questions of ultimate concern about death, afterlife, soul, and meaning in light of the Holocaust.

Images of the Afterlife in Shadows on the Hudson

Throughout the book Singer's deep familiarity with the full spectrum of afterlife beliefs in rabbinic and kabbalistic tradition is fully evident. One clear example is when Boris Makaver is reading the sacred text *Beginning of Wisdom (Reishit Hokhma)* by the kabbalist Elijah de Vidas. In his grandiosity, Boris thinks to himself that by reading this book his death would not be meaningless "material for another obituary notice, paid for with a few more dollars;"[278] rather:

> A soul is expected in the Upper World, where his deeds would be weighed with mercy and, after the obligatory punishment in Gehenna, he would attain Paradise [Gan Eden], where the secrets of Torah would be revealed to him and he would be led to glorious kingdoms and palaces, unlike anything known in this world.[279]

Here Singer alludes to very specific postmortem phenomena found in kabbalistic tradition: 1) The life review —"when God desires to take back a man's spirit, all the days he has lived in this world *pass in review* before Him" (Zohar, I, 221b); 2) Purification in Gehenna—"When the souls of the wicked leave this world many executioners of judgment await them and take them to Gehenna, and subject them there to three tortures every day. (Zohar, III, 70); and, 3) Visionary images of Gan Eden—"Every day the spirits of the righteous sit in rows in Gan Eden arrayed in their robes and praise God gloriously" (Zohar, I, 226b).

Clearly Singer knows his Jewish afterlife philosophy.

Similarly, another character, Dr. Alswanger, a scholar who had been a professor at Hebrew University in (pre-state) Israel, speculates about what happens after death, using traditional midrashic imagery, referring to *Hibbur HaKever*, the pangs of the grave, the postmortem state of confusion one potentially experiences upon death; guiding postmortem angels; and then the heavenly Garden of Eden, Gan Eden:

> It occurred to Dr. Alswangar that some-thing similar might well occur in the World to Come. First he would suffer, lie in agony, endure the torments of the grave, believing that the darkness, the worms, the oblivion would go on for-ever. But then suddenly angels would appear to him and lead him to a place where every soul had dignity and a name, where it received a welcome and an honor it had never known and never expected.[280]

Many characters in the book have lost loved ones in the Holocaust, and at Boris Makaver's dinner party there is banter going back and forth on postmortem survival and life after death. Professor David Shrage, a descendant of Hasidim, is a mathematician who studied in Switzerland and spent years devoted to psychic research. He "continued to mourn for [his wife] . . . and never ceased trying to contact her spirit in the world beyond."[281] Frieda Tamar, a learned woman and widow of a German Reform rabbi who perished at Auschwitz, cites Biblical texts in challenging Zadok Halperin, a cynical rationalist denigrating the idea of life after death. "'Zadok, don't forget that calling up the dead is recorded in Scripture,' Frieda called out. 'Saul went to a woman who had a familiar spirit and she summoned up the ghost of Samuel,'" she said, referring to the story in I Samuel 28.[282]

There are also the adventures of Henrietta Clark, formerly Chaye Sarah from the Buckovina, now a practicing dentist in Manhattan, and a psychic interested in spiritualism. Resonant with beliefs about the intercessory abilities of the deceased, she speaks about the interconnection between the living and the dead:

> We certainly need not fear those who in this life were dear and precious to us. They pray and intercede on our behalf. A thick wall separates Here from There, but when they are permitted for a brief while to make contact, there is absolutely no cause for any fear. All the spirits want is love and sympathy—not love of the body, of course, only love of the soul.[283]

Skepticism, Disbelief, and Modernity

In modernity a new voice of rational skepticism and materialist denial of any form of spirit, afterlife, or post-mortem survival emerged as a challenge to classical Jewish beliefs about life after death. Reflective of the emerging postwar Jewish consciousness, we see Boris Makaver—who changed his name from Borukh for the sake of business expediency—questioning his own beliefs:

> What if, God forbid, the unbelievers were right? The profane thought flashed through his mind. According to them, there was nothing: no God, no World to Come—merely atoms, electrons, blind forces. One was born and one died, to no purpose. Human beings were no better than dust. If they kill you, you're one more of the dead; of they let you live, you crawl around aimlessly . . . could this be the truth?[284]

Dialoguing on this topic with Dr. Solomon Margolin, Boris's old friend and yeshiva colleague in Europe, the dialectic between traditional faith, and post-Holocaust existential disbelief comes through: "We're machines, Borukh, blind automatons," says Dr. Margolin. In reply, Boris insists, "No, there is such a thing as a soul." Margolin continues, denigrating Torah, religion, notions of creation, and the like:

Where's the evidence for that? We've
built everything on some measly Pen-
tateuch penned by a petty scribe.
Afterward countless hacks pitched in
and added their two cents. None of
it has any connection with reality . . .
We've deluded ourselves that everything
must be created. Everything existed
from the beginning of eternity.[285]

Similarly, Stanislaw Luria, Boris's son-in-law, enters
into a conversation with Professor David Shrage, whose
wife had died in the Warsaw Ghetto, further articulating
the materialist rejection of traditional ideas of afterlife:

My own theory is that there is no spirit
whatever, because in the first place no
one has ever seen a spirit. In the second
place, where is it, this spirit? The earth
spins on its axis and revolves around the
sun. A spirit would have to spin around
with the earth, and thus be bound by
time and space. So it would cease to be
spirit . . . Neither you nor I have been to
heaven. Everything requires empirical
verification.[286]

After the Holocaust, the notion of a world without
God, soul, spirit, afterlife, a world without ultimate purpose or meaning—begins spreading, becoming part of
the normative cultural ambiance, and infusing itself into
the postwar Jewish *weltanschauung.* "Is God Dead?" asked

the iconic Time Magazine cover in April, 1966. With the hegemony of materialist science, rationalism and empirical verification replace religious belief and intuitive perception of non-visible realities. Singer excellently shows this in this novel.

Holocaust Trauma, Rejection of God, and the Death of Afterlife

Along with the spirit of materialism and rationalism, it was loss of faith after the Holocaust that catalyzed the progressive elimination of traditional Jewish beliefs in God, souls, and afterlife. After the Holocaust, it is much harder to think about the postmortem fate of death of six million souls. Singer skillfully portrays this rejection of old-world faith among the generation of Jews surviving the Holocaust genocide.

Esther, lover of Hertz Dovid Grein, an old friend of Boris Makaver, recounts the distressing story of a pious Jew in the ghettos of Nazi Europe, who spent his days and nights reciting Psalms. When they dragged away his family to the death camps, he continued his unending prayer and study, hiding somewhere in a cellar. "You know the justification: God know what He's doing. We sinned. In the World to Come we will make atonement."[287] This reflects ancient Biblical theology found in Ezek. 39:23: "The house of Israel went into exile for their iniquity; because they dealt treacherously against me, therefore I hid my face from them, and gave them to the hand of their enemies." Nearly starving to death, he sat in that cellar, with other Jews, waiting, hoping, praying . . . until he finally broke:

> Then one day he suddenly grabbed his phylacteries and tore them to pieces. He spat on them and he trampled them and he screamed, "God, I don't want to serve you any longer! You're worse than Hitler! I don't need you or your World to Come." So he destroyed everything—his fringed rituals undergarment and his prayer books, everything.[288]

This story epitomizes the impact of Holocaust on Jewish faith in the twentieth century. For many Jews of this era, the World to Come has come and gone. Afterlife and belief in God was of little use for those feeling traumatic shock and grief, abandoned by God. What had once been a meaningful theodicy—explanation for suffering through belief in afterlife and salvation in the World to Come—was wiped out, decimated, for a generation that witnessed the cruel extermination of human life in Nazi Germany.

In the voice of Stanislaw Luria, Isaac Bashevis Singer spoke what was the truth for so many of his generation. When David Shrage tells Luria, "We do not understand the mystery of suffering,"[289] Luria replies:

> What mystery can there be? For what purpose did God—if there is a God—need six million Jews to be wiped out in agonizing pain? And why was it necessary to burn children? Perhaps the adults had sinned, or God wanted to put them to the test. But what about the infants whose heads German officers smashed in? What about the children

who starved to death? What about the fathers who were forced to dig graves for themselves and their own children while the Nazis stood around and treated it all as a huge joke? What did God need this for?[290]

Why? Why? Why all this suffering? There is no answer. There is no longer a God one can believe in. And afterlife? Who can contemplate an afterlife of six million dead Jews?

Shadows on the Hudson is a novel of a collection of characters wrestling with love and sex, death and God. But more than this, it is a story of the shifting theological context of Jewish life in North America after the Holocaust. Unlike the other stories, plays, and novels presented in this book, this novel tells the story of the loss of belief in afterlife. And it was such loss of faith and belief which necessitated doing the spiritual archaeology to recover lost beliefs in postmortem survival that inspired and motivated writing a book such as this one.

So we have come full circle. Yes, Yiddish literature carried forth Jewish views of life after death, for over a century through the enlightenment, Haskalah, and modernity. But in the final analysis, in the second half of the twentieth century, Jews, particularly in the Western world, lost touch with sacred afterlife traditions. Now, in the twenty-first century, we have the opportunity to reclaim these lost traditions to provide meaning and comfort to those wrestling with the human encounter with death and loss. The Jewish legacy of afterlife teachings needs to be reincorporated into the contemporary corpus of death wisdom, as it was throughout many centuries of Jewish life.

8

Summary and Conclusions

Summary

We have traversed three centuries of Yiddish literature illuminating a panoply of images and themes of afterlife survival of the soul, and encountering a multi-tiered universe teeming with the shenanigans of otherworldly spirits and body-possessing dybbuks.

From one of the earliest selections of Yiddish writings—the seventeenth-century *Ma'aseh Book*—to *Shadows on the Hudson*—the post-Holocaust novel of Isaac Bashevis Singer—we see how classical Jewish afterlife teachings were presented and preserved through Yiddish literary lore. As the intellectual worldview of early modernity was being transformed by the emergence of Enlightenment rationalism and Haskalah secularism, Yiddish stories, novels, and plays kept alive and expressed traditional Jewish views of the hereafter.

To summarize the journey we have covered in the previous chapters of this book:

The *Ma'aseh Book* is an anonymously edited anthology of Yiddish folk literature with Jewish "ghost stories" depicting wandering spirits, discarnate beings, and tormenting dybbuks. The dybbuk tale in the *Ma'aseh Book*, the earliest printed story of this genre, tells of a disembodied being unable to enter Gehenna to engage in a postmortem purification process. Over the centuries, this story emerged as the paradigm for further stories of discarnate dybbukim (plural).

Being more of a rationalist than a mystic, the Yiddish author Sholem Aleichem did not chose to overtly explore life after death and postmortem survival as a literary theme. However, his *Tevye the Dairyman* stories end up forming the basis for stage and movie adaptations of *Fiddler on the Roof,* a beloved tale of the clash between traditional and modern values. In what might rightfully be one most famous scenes in all of Yiddish theater and cinema, deceased spirits appear in dreams from the world beyond and commune with the living. Through cultural translations and adaptations of *Fiddler on the Roof,* the arts have brought the ancient Jewish idea that the dead and the living can commune with each other to many corners of the globe.

The writings of Isaac Leib Peretz bridge the worlds of Haskalah and eighteenth-century Jewish socialist thought. His story "What is the Soul?" contains theological reflections on death and afterlife. The story "Bontshe Shvayg," one of the most beloved tales in all of Yiddish literature, is both a social critique of the oppressed Jewish masses of Eastern Europe and a creative depiction of a Heavenly Tribunal that replicates traditional rabbinic imagery. "Bontshe Shvayg" is a perfect example of how Peretz and his contemporaries blended the political philosophy of Yiddish culture with traditional rabbinic beliefs on postmortem reward and punishment.

S. An-sky's play *The Dybbuk, or Between Two Worlds,* dating from the early twentieth century, is an ageless story of star-crossed lovers, and has been performed on stage and in cinema for more than one hundred years. A gripping tale of dybbuk possession and exorcism mirroring historically documented cases of psychic attachment by vengeful, wayward spirits, *The Dybbuk* brought ancient kabbalistic thought about dybbuks and reincarnation (*gilgul*) to the contemporary Jewish world, Broadway, and the wider community.

The prolific writings of Isaac Bashevis Singer, whose life spanned almost the entire twentieth century, are replete with themes of death, afterlife, postmortem survival, and communication with spirits in the world beyond. His earliest novel, *Satan in Goray*, is a tale of dybbuk possession and mass hysteria in the age of the false Messiah Shabbatai Tzvi. "Sabbath in Gehenna" is a story weaving together Jewish philosophy of the afterlife with early modern political thought. And finally, *Shadows on the Hudson*, a story of Holocaust survivors rebuilding their lives in New York, chronicles the loss of faith and loss of belief in life after death after the Holocaust. Symbolically, as the last text delineated in this book, it highlights the emerging intellectual dialectic between faith and skepticism, and portrays the death of belief in the afterlife among Jews of the mid-twentieth century.

Conclusions

As this book demonstrates, the idea that Judaism does not hold a belief in life after death is not accurate at all. Today, we are living through a widespread cultural transformation of attitudes towards dying and death, and the emergence of new, creative approaches to end-of-life care. To put these changes taking place into context:

In 1900, Sigmund Freud's groundbreaking study *The Interpretation of Dreams* was published, which, in retrospect, inaugurated a widespread cultural transformation of attitudes towards human sexuality. And one hundred and twenty-five years later, we are still integrating and dealing with changing responses to human sexuality.

In 1969, Elisabeth Kübler-Ross's famed study *On Death and Dying* was published, which literally and symbolically catalyzed a process of transforming contemporary attitudes and approaches to death, dying and end-of-life care. In the past fifty-plus years, death and dying has "come out of the closet." Today we are still in the early stages of a complete revolution in the delivery of services for the dying and bereaved. Although widespread denial and discomfort in talking about death persists, the past half century has witnessed the proliferation of so many innovative approaches and transformative trends that are profoundly changing end-of-life care.

First of all, the earliest modern hospice was founded in England by Dame Cicely Saunders in 1967. Since then, hospice and palliative care have become a normal part of the medical world, with over nine thousand varied types of hospice programs in North America today. And there has also been a mushrooming of training programs for death doulas, who are finding employment both as private practitioners and in settings adjunct to the medical and hospital environment, to accompany people on the death-bed.

In funeral care, green burial and other environmentally friendly and sustainable methods of disposing of dead bodies are being developed. This includes human composting and alkaline hydrolysis (also known as water cremation) that breaks down the body using water and alkaline chemicals. With a global population of over eight million, these kinds of alternatives will continue to replace traditional in-ground burial.

Bereavement services have also become much more accessible. Besides the usual social work and hospice programs that offer support for families dealing with loss, many funeral homes now offer "after-care" services; and, additionally, there are hundreds of options for grief counseling, end-of-life care, and hospice support available online, transcending limitations of specific community and geography.

Two other emerging trends are profoundly transforming how we deal with death. The first is the proliferation of Medical Aid in Dying, a legal process for people with a terminal illness to choose to end their lives and reject often unneeded and unhelpful treatment interventions. Medical Aid in Dying is currently legal in Canada, New Zealand, some European and South American countries, and eleven American states. As it becomes more accepted and practiced ubiquitously, it will continue to transform end-of-life care. The other innovative trend is the use of psychedelic treatments for dying patients. Research being done at numerous locations in the United States and Canada is demonstrating that administering psilocybin, and other psychedelic substances, can help individuals with terminal diagnoses cope with and resolve the existential anxiety and fear of dying and death. Both of these trends will continue to expand in the coming decades, radically transforming death care.

Since the years of the COVID pandemic, the use of live-streaming and audio-visual conferencing for pastoral care and death and mourning rituals has become normative within our society. We have the resources to bring counseling, funeral rituals, shivah, Kaddish, and Yizkor services, bereavement groups, and other services to individuals and families in the comfort of their own homes. The Zoom revolution of end-of-life pastoral care is ongoing![291]

Several other trends and innovations bear mentioning. One such innovation has been Death Café and Death Over Dinner programs, whose open-ended explorations of individual and cultural responses to death are making conversations about death and dying more accessible to, and certainly attracting the interest of, millennials and Gen-Z. Another trend is the growing number of death and dying conferences and workshops exploring multifaceted dimensions of end-of-life care and traditions on afterlife and the survival of the soul after death. Additionally, thousands upon thousands of printed and audio-visual resources on death are now offered online. And lastly, among new books being published every day on death, dying, and grief, there is a resurgence of ancient Eastern and Indigenous wisdom traditions on dying and death. These bring a spiritual wisdom to death care, shifting the baseline of cultural awareness towards an understanding of both the finite nature of life and the eternality of the human soul.

Clearly, there is a lot going on to transform death and dying in our times, and this list is not exhaustive.

It is against this background that Jewish afterlife wisdom, found in Eastern European Yiddish culture and in Jewish mysticism and tradition, is contributing to the burgeoning cultural wisdom on death and afterlife and the growing transformation of attitudes towards dying and death.

In the final analysis, what we can extract from this study of spirits, ghosts and dybbuks in Yiddish lore is that between the world of the living and the world of the dead is a window, not a wall. While materialistic science assumes death as final and an impenetrable wall separating the dead and those left behind in embodied life, the wisdom of Jewish spirituality teaches that in our dreams, prayers, moments of quiet contemplation, and synchronistic moments of meaningful connection we can and do feel connected with loved ones on the other side of the window between life and death.

Throughout the ages, Judaism has taught that death is a sacred transition between this world and the world beyond. We live, life goes by quickly, and we die. In the brief passage of time that we are alive, Judaism encourages us to live life fully imbued with holiness and meaning. The wisdom found in age-old Jewish afterlife teachings—as we have discovered in our journey through the literary world of Yiddish culture—can inspire each of us to live life in fullness, in part by remaining in touch with the spirits of the dead and the ancestors watching over us at all times.

ENDNOTES

1. Joseph Naveh and Shaul Shaked, *Amulets and Magic Bowls: Aramaic Incantations of Late Antiquity* (Jerusalem: Magnes Press, 1987).

2. See, for example, Jean Herschaft, "Patient Should Not Be Told of Terminal Illness: Rabbi," *Jewish Post and Opinion*, March 13, 1981.

3. Zalman Schachter-Shalomi, "Foreword" to Simcha Paull Raphael, *Jewish Views of the Afterlife*, 3rd Ed. (Rowman and Littlefield, 2019), xix-xxvii.

4. Technically, in 1977 the school was known as California Institute of Asian Studies and was renamed California Institute of Integral Studies in 1980.

5. Simcha Steven Paull [Raphael], "Judaism's Contribution to the Psychology of Death and Dying" (PhD diss., California Institute of Integral Studies, 1986).

6. Shmuel Feiner, *The Origins of Jewish Secularization in Eighteenth-Century Europe* (University of Pennsylvania Press, 2010).

7. Raphael, *Jewish Views of the Afterlife*, 3rd Ed., 359-396.

8. Jean Baumgarten, *Introduction to Old Yiddish Literature*, ed. and tr. by Jerold C. Frakes (Oxford University Press, 2005), 26; Jeremy Dauber, *In the Demon's Bedroom: Yiddish Literature and the Early Modern Century* (Yale University Press, 2010), 5-6.

9. Chone Shmeruk, "Yiddish Literature," *Encyclopedia Judaica*, vol. 16, (Keter Publishing House, 1974), 798-833.

10. Baumgarten, *Introduction to Old Yiddish Literature*, vi.

11. Sol Liptzin, *The Flowering of Yiddish Literature* (Thomas Yoseloff, 1963), 131.

12. Sol Liptzin, *A History of Yiddish Literature* (Jonathan David Publishers, 1985), 7; According to Liptzin: "When this verse romance was reprinted in prose in the later half of the eighteenth century, its title was altered from Bovo-Bukh to Bovo-Maisse, 'maisse' being the Hebrew and Yiddish word for 'tale.' The similarity of 'Bovo' to 'Bobo,' the Yiddish designation for grandmother, led in the course of time to the

substitution of Bovo-Maisse for Bobo-Maisse and to the use of the former expression for any grandmother's tale or old-wives'-tale, with no necessary reference to to the original romance about the adventures of Sir Bovo."

13. Baumgarten, *Introduction to Old Yiddish Literature*, 315.

14. Jacob J. Maitlis, "Ma'aseh Book," *Encyclopedia Judaica*, vol. 11, 650-651; Moses Gaster, *Ma'aseh Book* (Jewish Publication Society, 1981); Raphael, *Jewish Views of the Afterlife*, 3rd ed., 241-243.

15. Charles Madison, *Yiddish Literature: Its Scope and Major Writers from Mendele and Sholom Aleichem to Isaac Bashevis Singer* (Schocken Books, 1971), vii

16. Liptzin, *A History of Yiddish Literature*, 38.

17. Olga Litvak, *The Romantic Movement in Judaism* (Rutgers University Press, 2012).

18. The Rabbinic material for the *Ma'aseh Book* was adapted from *Ein Yaakov*, a collection of legendary material of the Talmud, compiled by Rabbi Yaakov ibn Chaviv, the fifteenth-century talmudist. The most accessible compilation of these stories in English is the translation done by Moses Gaster in his *Ma'aseh Book*. A near-complete online compilation of these stories, using Gaster's translation, with Hebrew commentary on known sources of the stories, was done by Yoel Peretz and can be accessed at folkmasa.org/mb/b0mavo.htm.

19. According to Baumgarten, hagiographical stories about *Hasidei Ashkenaz*, "constitute a homogeneous collection on which the compiler based his work and which he incorporated as a whole into the Maase-bukh. [As one of the tales in this selection] reads: "Now I would like to begin to write stories of R. Judah and his father, R. Samuel the Pious, and that which took place during their time." Baumgarten, *Introduction to Old Yiddish Literature*, 307.

20. Maitlis, "Ma'aseh Book," 650-651; Meyer Waxman, *A History of Jewish Literature*, vol. II (Thomas Yoseloff, 1960), 656.

21. See Morris Faierstein, "The Dibbuk in the *Mayse Bukh*," *Shofar: An Interdisciplinary Journal of Jewish Studies* 30, no.1 (2011), 94-103.

22. Talmud, Bava Metzia, 84b.

23. Gaster, *Ma'aseh Book*, no.125—"The Death of Rabbi and His Home Visits on Friday Nights," 223.

24. Talmud, Berachot, 18b.

25. Gaster, *Ma'aseh Book*, no. 121—"Zeiri and the Dead Hostess," 217.

26. Joshua Trachtenberg, *Jewish Magic and Superstition: A Study in Folk Religion* (Athenum, 1974), 223-224.

27. Pinchas Giller, "Recovering the Sanctity of the Galilee: The Veneration of Sacred Relics in Classical Kabbalah," *Journal of Jewish Thought and Philosophy* 4, no.1 (1995), 147-169; J.H. Chajes, *Between Worlds: Dybbuks, Exorcists and Early Modern Judaism* (University of Pennsylvania Press, 2003), 21; Elliott Horowitz, "Speaking to the Dead: Cemetery Prayer in Medieval and Early Modern Jewry," *The Journal of Jewish Thought and Philosophy* 8, no.1 (1999), 303-317.

28. Stefanie Halpern, "A Meeting of Life and Death: Ritual and Performance at the Ohel, the Grave of Rabbi Menachem Mendel Schneerson," *Journal of Ritual Studies* 29, no. 1 (2015), 21-34.

29. Issachar Ben-Ami, *Saint Veneration Among the Jews in Morocco* (Wayne State University Press, 1998), 93-104.

30. Susan Starr Sered, "Rachel's Tomb: The Development of a Cult," *Jewish Studies Quarterly* 2, no. 2 (1995),103-148.

31. Gaster, *Ma'aseh Book*, no. 88—"Of The Wicked Tax Gatherer and the Learned Rabbi Whose Bodies Were Inter-Changed at the Funeral," 146.

32. Gaster, *Ma'aseh Book*, 147.

33. Trachtenberg, *Jewish Magic and Superstition*, 234.

34. Yehudah HeChasid, *Sefer Chasidim: The Book of the Pious by Rabbi Yehudah HeChasid*, ed. Avraham Yaakov Finkel (Jason Aronson Inc., 1997), 340-344; See also, Issachar Ben-Ami, *Saint Veneration*, 85-92.

35. For a contemporary perspective on dream visitations, see Susan Olson, *Images of the Dead in Grief Dreams: A Jungian View of Mourning*, 2nd ed. (Routledge, 2021).

36. Gaster, *Ma'aseh Book*, no. 251—"Story of a Man Who Rose Alone at Night and Saw a Whole Army of Dead People Pulling Wagons Full of Other Dead People," 654.

37. Gaster, *Ma'aseh Book*, no. 252—"The Dead Man Who Was Driven around a Field Which He had Unjustly Appropriated in Life," 655.

38. Gaster, *Ma'aseh Book*, no. 214—"The Corpse and the Torn Sleeve," 521-523.

39. Ibid., 523.

40. A similar literary construction can be found in Hasidic tales, for example in a story told of Reb Elimelech of Lyzensk, where a disembodied spirit reports to Reb Elimelech that: "At the moment of death I did not feel any pain. It was like taking a hair from milk." Martin Buber, *Tales of the Hasidim: Later Masters* vol. II (Schocken Books, 1977), 94-95. This directly quotes the Talmudic passages Berachot 8a and Moed Katan 28a using this metaphor to describe the effortlessness of death.

41. Gedalyah Nigel, *Magic, Mysticism and Hasidism: The Supernatural in Jewish Thought*, trans. Edward Levin (Jason Aronson, 1994), 263.

42. Gaster, *Ma'aseh Book*, no. 152—"The Dibbuk," 301-303.

43. Joachim Neugroschel, *The Dybbuk and the Yiddish Imagination: A Haunted Reader* (Syracuse University Press, 2000), 59; Morris Faierstein has shown that the dybbuk story in the *Ma'aseh Book* is adapted from a handwritten letter of R. Elijah Falco, distributed in Safed, in 1571. The original letter, or a modified version thereof, made its way to the editor of the *Ma'aseh Book* who presents a more sanitized version of the Safed-based story. See, Faierstein, "The Dibbuk in the *Mayse Bukh*," 97-98.

44. Faierstein, ibid., 96.

45. Ibid.

46. See Neugroschel, *The Dybbuk and the Yiddish Imagination*, and Gershon Winkler, *Dybbuk* (Judaica Press, 1982).

47. For a fuller explication of the Kabbalistic notion of *gilgul*, see Raphael, *Jewish Views of the Afterlife*, 3rd ed., 224-239.

48. *Agunah*, literally 'anchored' or 'chained,' is a halakhic term describing a Jewish woman who is 'chained' to her marriage, historically because a man has left on a journey or went to war and not returned. Today it is the term used to describe a woman who cannot receive a '*get*,' a religious divorce from her husband, and hence cannot remarry.

49. Gaster, *Ma'aseh Book*, 301.

50. Ibid., 301-302.

51. Fernando Peñasola, *The Dybbuk: Text, Subtext, and Context* (Tsiterboym Books, 2012), 51-52.

52. Gaster, *Ma'aseh Book*, 302-303.

53. Ibid., 303.

54. Gershom Scholem, *Kabbalah* (New American Library, 1978), 347.

55. Chaim Vital, *Shaar HaMitzvot, Ekev*, Fol. 41b-42a, cited by Moshe Hallamish, *An Introduction to the Kabbalah*, trans. Ruth Bar-Ilan and Ora Wiskind-Elper (State University of New York Press, 1999), 301.

56. Ibid.

57. Ken Frieden, *Classic Yiddish Fiction: Abramovitsh, Sholem Aleichem, and Peretz* (State University of New York Press, 1995), 109.

58. Ibid.

59. Ibid.

60. Dan Miron, "Sholem Aleichem," *Encyclopedia Judaica*, vol. 14, 1271-1286.

61. Jeremy Dauber, *The Worlds of Sholem Aleichem: The Remarkable Life and Afterlife of the Man Who Created Tevye* (Schocken Books, 2013), 5.

62. Miron, "Sholem Aleichem," 1278; Wayne Hoffman, "A 'Fiddler' in Tokyo," Tablet, January 8, 2018, tabletmag.com/sections/news/articles/a-fiddler-in-tokyo

63. Dauber, *The Worlds of Sholem Aleichem*, 4.

64. Miron, "Sholem Aleichem," 1285.

65. Ibid.

66. Waxman, *A History of Jewish Literature*, vol. IV, 512.

67. Frieden, *Classic Yiddish Fiction*, 161.

68. Ibid., 159.

69. Sholem Aleichem, *Tevye the Dairyman and the Railroad Stories*, trans. Hillel Halkin (Schocken Books, 1987), xvii.

70. The third, fourth, fifth and eighth in Hillel Halkin's translation of *Tevye the Dairyman and the Railroad Stories*.

71. Aleichem, *Tevye the Dairyman and the Railroad Stories*, 50.

72. See Frederick Thomas Elworthy, *The Evil Eye: The Classic Account of an Ancient Superstition* (Dover Publications, 2004), 412-ff.

73. Aleichem, *Tevye the Dairyman and the Railroad Stories*, 50-51.

74. Ibid., 51.

75. Ibid., 52.

76. J. Hoberman, *Bridge of Light: Yiddish Film Between Two Worlds* (Temple University Press, 1995), 53-54.

77. Dauber, *The Worlds of Sholem Aleichem*, 4. See also Miron, "Sholem Aleichem,"1285-1286.

78. Dauber, *The Worlds of Sholem Aleichem*, 4.

79. Leo Wiener, *History of Yiddish Literature in the Nineteenth Century*, 2nd edition (Herman Press, 1972), 111.

80. Frieden, *Classic Yiddish Fiction*, 253.

81. Liptzin, *Flowering of Yiddish Literature*, 58.

82. Ibid.

83. Waxman, *Jewish Literature*, vol. IV, 495.

84. Liptzin, *Flowering of Yiddish Literature*, 103.

85. Ibid., 62ff.

86. Ibid., 56.

87. Ruth R. Wisse, "Peretz, Yitskhok Leybush," *YIVO Encyclopedia of Jews in Eastern Europe*, Accessed July 25, 2025, yivoencyclopedia. org/article.aspx/Peretz_Yitskhok_Leybush.

88. Wisse, "Introduction" in *The I.L. Peretz Reader* by I.L Peretz (Schocken Books, 1990), xiii.

89. Not discussed in this chapter is a third story, "Yom Kippur in Hell" (alternately translated as "Neilah in Gehenna"), published in 1915 at the end of Peretz's life.

90. Peretz, "What is the soul?" in *The I.L. Peretz Reader*, 93.

91. Ibid.

92. Yechiel Michal Tucazinsky, *Sefer Gesher HaHayyim* (n.p., 1960), I, 3:2.

93. Peretz, "What is the Soul?", 93.

94. *Mahzor Vitry*, ed. Aryeh Goldschmidt (Jerusalem: Or HaMizrah, 2003), 223, quoted by David I. Shyovitz, "You Have Saved Me From the Judgment of Gehenna: The Origins of the Kaddish in Medieval Ashkenaz" *AJS Review* 39, no. 1 (April 2015), 49–73. For discussion on the psychospiritual import of Kaddish, see Raphael, *Jewish Views of the Afterlife*, 3rd ed., 387-389. See also Leon Wiesltier, *Kaddish* (Knopf Doubleday Publishing Group, 2000).

95. There is ancient lore associating birds with survival beyond death and the flight of human souls. See Brian Taylor, "Taking Soul Birds Seriously: A Post-Secular Animist Perspective on Extra-Ordinary Communications" *Paranthropology: Anthropological Approaches to the Paranormal* 6, no. 2 (July 2015).

96. Peretz, "What is the Soul?", 94.

97. Ibid.

98. Ibid.

99. Ibid.

100. See Raphael, *Jewish Views of the Afterlife*, 3rd ed., 313.

101. Peretz, "What is the Soul?", 96.

102. Contemporary psychological studies demonstrate the possibility of fetal consciousness and memory. See Thomas Verney and John Kelly, *The Secret Life of the Unborn Child: How You Can Prepare Your Unborn Baby for a Happy, Healthy Life* (Bantam Dell Publishing, 1981).

103. J. D. Eisenstein, ed., *Otzar Midrashim*, vol. 1, (Grossman, 1915), 243; translation adapted from Raphael Patai, *Gates to the Old City* (Jason Aronson, 1998), 378–81.

104. W. Hirsch, *Rabbinic Psychology—Beliefs about the Soul in Rabbinic Literature of the Talmudic Period* (Edward Goldstone, 1947), 150-174.

105. Shabbat 152b; Pesikta Rabbati 2:3.

106. Peretz, "What is the Soul?", 96.

107. Ibid., 99.

108. Ibid.

109. Ibid., 100.

110. Ibid. According to the Zohar, fire represents the quality of human passion, and the burning fires of hell [Gehenna] "corresponds to the hot passion of sinfulness in man" (II, 150b).

111. Peretz, "What is the Soul?", 101

112. Ibid.

113. Ibid.,103.

114. Ibid.

115. Ibid.

116. Ibid.,104.

117. Ibid.

118. Peretz, "Bontshe Shvayg" in *The I.L. Peretz Reader*, 146.

119. Leo Tolstoy, *Death of Ivan Illych*, trans. Lynn Solotaroff (Bantam Books, 1981).

120. Wiener, *History of Yiddish Literature in the Nineteenth Century*, 333ff.

121. Peretz, "Bontshe Shvayg," 146.

122. Ibid., 147.

123. Ibid., 146.

124. Ibid., 147.

125. See the selection of medieval Midrashic Gan Eden texts in Raphael, *Jewish Views of the Afterlife*, 3rd ed., 143-160.

126. Peretz, "Bontshe Shvayg," 147.

127. Ibid.,148.

128. Ibid.

129. Ibid.,149

130. Ibid., 151.

131. Ibid.

132. Ibid.,151-152.

133. Ibid.,152

134. Ibid.

135. Ibid.

136. Ibid.

137. Hermann Cohen, *Religion of Reason out of the Sources of Judaism*, trans. Simon Kaplan (Frederick Unger Publishing, 1972), 301.

138. Gabriella Safran and Steven J. Zipperstein, eds., *The Worlds of S. An-sky: A Russian Jewish Intellectual at the Turn of the Century*, (Stanford University Press, 2006), 3ff.; Peñasola, *The Dybbuk*, 1-2.

139. David G. Roskies, "Introduction" in *The Dybbuk and Other Writings* by S. An-sky, trans. Golda Werman (Yale University Press, 2002), xvii.

140. Gabriella Safran, *Wandering Soul: The Dybbuk's Creator—S. An-sky* (Harvard University Press, 2010), 204.

141. Most of An-sky's personal and professional papers were inaccessible until after the fall of communism in the 1980's. Safran and Zipperstein, *The Worlds of S. An-sky*, 15.

142. Peñasola, *The Dybbuk*, 24.

143. Agnieszka Legutko, "Possessed by the Other: Dybbuk Possession and Modern Jewish Identity in Twentieth-Century Jewish Literature and Beyond," (PhD Diss., Columbia University, 2012),71.

144. Safran and Zipperstein, *The Worlds of S. An-sky,* 23.

145. *Der Dibuk,* directed by Michal Waszynski (Poland: 1937; 123 minutes; Yiddish with new English subtitles), based on the play by S. An-sky, National Center for Jewish Film, youtube.com/watch?v=AVThFw1xx1o.

146. Agnieszka Legutko lists over one hundred productions inspired by and adapted from An-sky's (Legutko, *The Dybbuk, Or Between Two Worlds,* 248-281).

147. According to Rachel Elior, An-sky's Jewish sources include: *Sippur dibbuk,* a dybbuk narrative from the 18th century, *Ma'asiyah nora'ah*; tales of Reb Nahman of Bratslav; tales of *Kehal hasidim* and *Sippir ha-betulah mi-ludmir,* the story of the maid Ludmir, who is said to have refused to marry her betrothed groom (Rachel Elior, *Dybbuks and Jewish Women in Social History, Mysticism and Folklore* (Urim Publications, 2008),112).

148. For background on Shabbatai Tzvi, see Gershom Scholem, *Sabbatai Sevi: The Mystical Messiah, 1626–1676,* trans. Zvi Werblowsky (Princeton University Press, 2016).

149. Ruthie Abeliovich, "The Dybbuk before *The Dybbuk*" in *The Dybbuk Century: The Play That Possessed the World* edited by Debra Caplan and Rachel Merrill Moss (University of Michigan Press, 2023), 16.

150. S. An-sky, "Death in Jewish Folk Belief" (in Yiddish) *Filologishe shrift fun YIVO 3* (1929), 90-100, quoted by Roskies in *The Dybbuk and Other Writings,* xxiv-xxv. A complete description of An-sky's ethnographic questionnaire is found in Daniel Deutsch, *The Jewish Dark Continent - Life and Death in the Russian Pale of Settlement* (Harvard University Press, 2011), 103-313.

151. Quoted by Peñasola in *The Dybbuk,* 13.

152. Nathan Hanover, *The Abyss of Despair (Yeven Metzulah): The Famous 17th Century Chronicle Depicting Jewish Life in Russia and Poland during the Chmielnicki Massacres of 1648-1649,* trans. Abraham J. Mesch (Transaction Publishers, 1983).

153. Peñasola, *The Dybbuk*, 24.

154. *The Dybbuk*, directed by Sidney Lumet, originally broadcast October 3rd, 1960, NTA Film Network. DVD, The Archive of American Television.

155. S. An-sky, *A Dybbuk and Other Tales of the Supernatural*, adapted by Tony Kushner, trans. Joachim Neugroschel (Theater Communications Group, 1998); Charles Isherwood, "A Dybbuk, or Between Two Worlds," *Variety*, November 29th, 1997.

156. Dan Pine, "Feminist Twist on Yiddish Classic in Operatic Dybbuk," Jewish News of Northern California, September 16th, 2016. The Israeli composer Ofer Ben-Amots has recast *The Dybbuk* as a multimedia English and Hebrew chamber opera which has been performed as recently as 2016 (vimeo.com/181570317).

157. Elior, *Dybbuks and Jewish Women*, 122.

158. Joseph Dan, "Raziel, Book of," *Encyclopedia Judaica*, vol. 13, 1592-1593.

159. See Scholem, *Sabbatai Sevi*.

160. An-sky, *The Dybbuk and Other Writings*, 34.

161. Chajes, *Between Worlds*, 81.

162. For primary source descriptions of five sixteenth-century Jewish exorcism rituals, see Daniel R. Shevitz, "Rituals for Jewish Exorcism" in *The Jewish Almanac*, eds. Richard Siegel and Carl Rheins (Bantam Books, 1980), 568-572.

163. Psalm 68:1, Num. 10:35.

164. An-sky, *The Dybbuk and Other Writings*, 46.

165. Ibid., 49.

166. Ibid.

167. Ibid.

168. Tzvi Yivrov, *L'illui Neshamah* (B'nai Brak: 2008), 15. See also Nadya Gross and Raphael, Simcha Paull, "In Preparation For Yizkor: Opening The Window To Loved Ones In The World Beyond," *Evolve—Groundbreaking Jewish Conversations*, September

29, 2024, evolve.reconstructingjudaism.org/in-preparation-for-yizkor-opening-the-window-to-loved-ones-in-the-world-beyond/.

169. An-sky, *The Dybbuk and Other Writings*, 49.

170. Trachtenberg, *Jewish Magic and Superstition*, 62.

171. An-sky, *The Dybbuk and Other Writings*, 49.

172. See endnote #144

173. Gabriella Safran, "Dancing with Death and Salvaging Jewish Culture in Austria and The Dybbuk," *Slavic Review* 59, no. 4 (2000), 761–81.

174. An-sky, *The Dybbuk and Other Writings*, 21.

175. Ibid.

176. Ibid., 23

177. See Herman Pollack, *Jewish Folkways in Germanic Lands (1648-1806): Studies in Aspects of Daily Life* (MIT Press, 1971), 38. Michael Alpert, "Freylekhs on Film: The Portrayal of Jewish Traditional Dance in Yiddish Cinema," *Jewish Folklore and Ethnology Newsletter* 8, no. 3-4, 1986, 5-6, 35.

178. Elior, *Dybbuks and Jewish Women*, 111.

179. Alpert, "Freylekhs on Film . . .," 7.

180. An-sky, *The Dybbuk and Other Writings*, 24.

181. Ibid.

182. Ibid.

183. Ibid.

184. Ibid., 25.

185. Raphael, *Jewish Views of the Afterlife*, 3rd ed., 229-230.

186. An-sky, *The Dybbuk and Other Writings*, 25.

187. Samuel H. Dresner, *The Zaddik: The Doctrine of the Zaddik According to the Writings of Rabbi Yaakov Yosef of Polnoy* (Jason Aronson Publishers, 1977).

188. An-sky, *The Dybbuk and Other Writings*, 25-26

189. Ibid.

190. Dozens of primary sources document exorcism stories in Kabbalistic and, especially, Hasidic literature. See Nigel, *Magic, Mysticism and Hasidism*, 263, n. 402.

191. Ibid.,112-114.

192. Chajes, *Between Worlds*, 81.

193. An-sky, *The Dybbuk and Other Writings*, 35.

194. Tamar Alexander, "Love and Death in a Contemporary *Dybbuk* Story: Personal Narrative and the Female Voice" in *Spirit Possession in Judaism*, ed. Matt Goldish, 314.

195. An-sky, *The Dybbuk and Other Writings*, 36.

196. Ibid., 36-37.

197. Ibid., 37.

198. Elior, *Dybbuks and Jewish Women*, 104

199. Ibid., 94.

200. Ibid.

201. Jacob Emden, *Siddur Beit Yakov*, originally published Altona, 1745-48, (Otzar Hasefarim, n.d.), 132-135. See also H.A. Addison, "I Have Dreamed a Dream" in *Birkat Kohanim: The Priestly Benediction*, eds. D. Birnbaum and Martin S. Cohen (New Paradigm Matrix Publishing, 2016), 341-364.

202. Emden, *Siddur Beit Yakov*, 132-135.

203. S. Ansky, *The Dybbuk and Other Writings*,40.

204. Ibid., 41.

205. In I Sam. 28:7-25, King Saul asks the Witch of Endor (*aishet ba'alat ob*) to commune on his behalf with the spirit of his deceased mentor, Samuel the Prophet. She can see Samuel, King Saul can hear him, what we may call clairvoyance and clairaudience.

206. S. An-sky, *The Dybbuk and Other Writings*, 45

207. Chajes, *Between Worlds*, 65-66.

208. Psalm 68:1, Num. 10:35.

209. An-sky, *The Dybbuk and Other Writings*, 46.

210. Ibid., 49.

211. Ibid.

212. Ibid.

213. Ruth R. Wisse, "Introduction" in *Satan in Goray* by Isaac Bashevis Singer, trans. A.H. Gross (Farrar, Straus and Giroux, 1996), xv.

214. Leonard Pragar, "Bashevis Singer, Isaac," *Encyclopedia Judaica*, vol. 4, 294-295.

215. Julia St. Vrain French, "In the Face of A Silent God: Isaac Bashevis Singer's Jews—The Pious, the Profane, and the Irresolute," (Master's Thesis, California State University Dominguez Hills, 2000), 147-161.

216. Isaac Bashevis Singer, *In My Father's Court* (Signet Books, 1967), 17

217. Isaac Bashevis Singer, *A Little Boy in Search of God or Mysticism in a Personal Light* (Doubleday, 1976), 1553; Wisse, "Introduction" in *Satan in Goray*, xxv.

218. Grace Farrell-Lee, *From Exile to Redemption : The Fiction of Isaac Bashevis Singer* (Southern Illinois University Press, 1987), 12-ff.

219. Isaac Bashevis Singer, *The Magician of Lublin*, trans. Elaine Gottlieb and Joseph Singer (Farrar, Straus and Giroux, 1960), 278.

220. Isaac Bashevis Singer, *The Family Moskat*, trans. A.H. Gross (Farrar, Straus and Giroux, 1950), 607.

221. Elzbieta Domanska, "Influence of Cabala on the Adult Short Stories of Isaac Bashevis Singer" (Masters Thesis, Emporia State University, 2001), 54ff.

222. Cited by French in *In the Face of A Silent God*, 53-54.

223. Singer, *Satan in Goray*, 4.

224. See Scholem, *Sabbatai Sevi*.

225. Wisse, "Introduction" in *Satan in Goray*, xxviii.

226. Singer, *Satan in Goray*, 211-217

227. Ibid., 219-239

228. Wisse, "Introduction" in *Satan in Goray*, 56.

229. Ibid., 57.

230. Ibid., 62.

231. Solomon Ganzfried, *Kitzur Shulchan Arukh*, trans. Hyman E. Goldin (Hebrew Publishing Co. 1964), vol. 4, ch. 194, p. 90.

232. Singer, *Satan in Goray*, 65

233. Ibid.

234. Ibid., 66.

235. See Abner Weiss, *Death and Bereavement : A Halakhic Guide* (Ktav Publishing House, Inc., 1991), 156-158.

236. Ibid., 177.

237. Chava Weissler, "The Traditional Piety of Ashkenazic Women" in *Jewish Spirituality Vol. 2: From the Sixteenth Century Revival to the Present*, ed. Arthur Green (Crossroad Publishing, 1987), 263.

238. See *Spirit Possession in Judaism*, ed. Matt Goldish, 367-444.

239. Singer, *Satan in Goray*, 156.

240. Ibid., 203.

241. Ibid., 217.

242. Ibid., 224.

243. Ibid., 225-226.

244. Raphael, *Jewish Views of the Afterlife*, 3rd ed., 209-210.

245. Ibid.; Zalman Schachter-Shalomi, "Life in the Hereafter: A Tour of What's to Come" in *The Jewish Almanac*, eds. Richard Siegel and Carl Rheins (Bantam Books, 1980), 594–96.

246. Raphael, *Jewish Views of the Afterlife*, 3rd ed., 209-210

247. Singer, *Satan in Goray*, 232.

248. Ibid., 227

249. Ibid., 234.

250. Ibid., 235-236.

251. Ibid., 236.

252. Tzvi Freeman, "Kaddish Eases Judgment and Elevates the Soul," Chabad.org, Accessed July 25th, 2025, chabad.org/library/article_cdo/aid/282567/jewish/Judgment-and-Elevation.htm

253. Singer, *Satan in Goray*, 236.

254. Ibid., 238.

255. Ibid., 239.

256. It was published in "Summary Bibliography: Isaac Bashevis Singer" in the Yiddish newspaper *Forverts* [The Jewish Daily Forward], December 16th, 1972, accessed August 11th, 2018, isfdb.org/cgi-bin/title.cgi?2294680.

257. Isaac Bashevis Singer, "Sabbath in Gehenna" in *The Death of Methuselah and Other Stories*, (Faffar, Straus and Giroux,1988).

258. Ibid., 212.

259. Ibid.

260. *Beit Ha-Midrash*, vol. I, ed. Adolph Jellinek (Jerusalem: Wahrman Books, 1967), 148-149; Raphael, *Jewish Views of the Afterlife*, 3rd ed., 139.

261. Singer, "Sabbath in Gehenna," 212.

262. See Neil Gillman, *The Death of Death: Resurrection and Immortality in Jewish Thought* (Jewish Lights Publishing, 1997); Raphael, *Jewish Views of the Afterlife;* Zachary Alan Starr, *Toward A History of Jewish Thought: The Soul, Resurrection, and the Afterlife* (Wipf and Stock, 2020).

263. S. Ettinger, "The Socialist Movement Among Jews Before the First World War" in *A History of the Jewish People*, ed. H.H. Ben-Sasson (Harvard University Press, 1976), 908-914.

264. Singer, "Sabbath in Gehenna," 213.

265. Ibid., 213-214.

266. Shabbat 33b

267. Singer, "Sabbath in Gehenna," 214.

268. Ibid., 215.

269. Ibid., 216-217.

270. Ibid., 218.

271. Understood to be the reality life before death, death being a transition into the real world of postmortem life.

272. Singer, "Sabbath in Gehenna," 218.

273. Ibid.

274. Ibid., 219

275. Isaac Bashevis Singer, *Shadows on the Hudson*, trans. Joseph Sherman (Farrar, Straus and Giroux, 1998).

276. Sean Warsch, "A 'holocaust' Becomes 'the Holocaust,'" *Jewish Magazine*, October, 2006, http://www.jewishmag.com/107mag/holocaustword/holocaustword.htm.

277. Richard Bernstein, "'Shadows on the Hudson:' Dark Side of Isaac Bashevis Singer," *New York Times*, December 31st, 1997.

278. Singer, *Shadows on the Hudson*, 393

279. Ibid., 393-394.

280. Ibid., 278.

281. Ibid., 11.

282. See my discussion of this passage in *Jewish Views of the Afterlife*, 3rd ed., 13-14, 40.

283. Singer, *Shadows on the Hudson*, 266; David Malkiel, "Between Worldliness and Traditionalism: Eighteenth-Century Jews Debate Intercessory Prayer," *Jewish Studies: an Internet Journal* 2 (2003), 169-198.

284. Ibid., 489.

285. Ibid., 335.

286. Ibid., 133.

287. Singer, *Shadows on the Hudson*, 102

288. Ibid.

289. Ibid.,135.

290. Ibid.

291. See Simcha Raphael, Dayle A. Friedman, and David Levin, eds., *Jewish End-of-Life Care in a Virtual Age: Our Traditions Reimagined* (Albion-Andalus Books, 2021).

Bibliography

Abeliovich, Ruthie. "The Dybbuk before *The Dybbuk*." In *The Dybbuk Century: The Play That Possessed the World*, edited by Debra Caplan and Rachel Merrill Moss. University of Michigan Press, 2023.

Addison, H. A. "I Have Dreamed a Dream." In *Birkat Kohanim: The Priestly Benediction*, edited by D. Birnbaum and M. S. Cohen. New Paradigm Matrix, 2016.

Aleichem, Sholem. *Tevye the Dairyman and the Railroad Stories*. Translated by Hillel Halkin. Schocken Books, 1987.

Alpert, Michael. "Freylekhs on Film: The Portrayal of Jewish Traditional Dance in Yiddish Cinema." *Jewish Folklore and Ethnology Newsletter* 8, no. 3-4 (1986): 5-6, 35.

An-sky, S. *A Dybbuk and Other Tales of the Supernatural*, adapted by Tony Kushner. Translated by Joachim Neugroschel. Theater Communications Group, 1998.

———. "Death in Jewish Folk Belief" (in Yiddish) *Filologishe shrift fun YIVO* 3 (1929): 90-100

———. *The Dybbuk and Other Writings*. Edited by David G. Roskies. Translated by Golda Werman. Yale University Press, 2002.

Baumgarten, Jean. *Introduction to Old Yiddish Literature*. Edited and Translated by Jerold C. Frakes. Oxford University Press, 2005.

Ben-Ami, Issachar, *Saint Veneration Among the Jews in Morocco*. Wayne State University Press, 1998.

Bernstein, Richard. "'Shadows on the Hudson:' Dark Side of Isaac Bashevis Singer." *New York Times*, December 31st, 1997.

Buber, Martin. *Tales of the Hasidim, Vol. II: The Later Masters*. Schocken Books, 1977.

Cohen, Hermann. *Religion of Reason out of the Sources of Judaism.* Translated by Simon Kaplan. Frederick Unger Publishing, 1972.

Chajes, J.H, *Between Worlds: Dybbuks, Exorcists and Early Modern Judaism.* University of Pennsylvania Press, 2003.

Dauber, Jeremy. *In the Demon's Bedroom—Yiddish Literature and the Early Modern Century.* Yale University Press, 2010.

———. *The Worlds of Sholem Aleichem—The Remarkable Life and Afterlife of the Man Who Created Tevye.* Schocken Books, 2013.

Deutsch, Daniel. *The Jewish Dark Continent: Life and Death in the Russian Pale of Settlement.* Harvard University Press, 2011.

Dresner, Samuel H. *The Zaddik: The Doctrine of the Zaddik According to the Writings of Rabbi Yaakov Yosef of Polnoy.* Jason Aronson, 1977.

Eisenstein, J.D., ed. *Otzar Midrashim.* Vol. I. Grossman, 1915.

Elior, Rachel. *Dybbuks and Jewish Women in Social History, Mysticism and Folklore.* Urim Publications, 2008.

Elworthy, Frederick Thomas. *The Evil Eye : The Classic Account of an Ancient Superstition.* Dover Publications, 2004.

Encyclopaedia Judaica. Macmillan, 1971.

Ettinger, S. "The Socialist Movement Among Jews Before the First World War" in *A History of the Jewish People.* Edited by H.H. Ben-Sasson. Harvard University Press, 1976.

Faierstein, Morris M. "The Dibbuk in the Mayse Bukh." *Shofar: An Interdisciplinary Journal of Jewish Studies* 30, no. 1 (2011): 94-103

———. *The Dybbuk: Its Origins and History.* SUNY Press, 2024.

———. "The Dybbuk: The Origins and History of a Concept." In *Olam Ha-zeh V'olam Ha-ba: This World and the World to Come in Jewish Belief and Practice.* Edited by Leonard J. Greenspoon. Purdue University Press, 2017.

French, Julia St. Vrain. "In the Face of A Silent God: Isaac Bashevis Singer's Jews : The Pious, the Profane, and the Irresolute." Masters Thesis, California State University Dominguez Hills, 2000.

Frieden, Ken. *Classic Yiddish Fiction: Abramovitsh, Sholem Aleichem, and Peretz.* State University of New York Press, 1995.

Ganzfried, Solomon. *Kitzur Shukhan Arukh.* Translated by Hyman E. Goldin. Hebrew Publishing Co., 1964.

Giller, Pinchas. "Recovering the Sanctity of the Galilee: The Veneration of Gravesites in Classical Kabbalah." *Journal of Jewish Thought and Philosophy* 4 (1994): 147-69.

Gillman, Neil. *The Death of Death: Resurrection and Immortality in Jewish Thought.* Jewish Lights Publishing, 1997.

Grace, Farrell-Lee. *From Exile to Redemption: The Fiction of Isaac Bashevis Singer.* Southern Illinois University Press, 1987

Gross, Nadya and Raphael, Simcha Paull, "In Preparation For Yizkor: Opening The Window To Loved Ones In The World Beyond." *Evolve—Groundbreaking Jewish Conversations.* September 29th, 2024. evolve.reconstructingjudaism.org/in-preparation-for-yizkor-opening-the-window-to-loved-ones-in-the-world-beyond/

Halpern, Stefanie. "A Meeting of Life and Death: Ritual and Performance at the Ohel, the Grave of Rabbi Menachem Mendel Schneerson." *Journal of Ritual Studies* 29, No. 1 (2015): 21-34

Hanover, Nathan. *The Abyss of Despair (Yeven Metzulah): The Famous 17th Century Chronicle Depicting Jewish Life in Russia and Poland during the Chmielnicki Massacres of 1648-1649.* Translated by Abraham J. Mesch. Transaction Publishers, 1983.

HeChasid, Yehudah. *Sefer Chasidim: The Book of the Pious by Rabbi Yehudah HeChasid.* Edited and Translated by Avraham Yaakov Finkel. Jason Aronson Inc., 1997.

Herschaft, Jean. "Patient Should Not Be Told of Terminal Illness: Rabbi." *Jewish Post and Opinion*. March 13th, 1981.

Hirsch, W. *Rabbinic Psychology—Beliefs about the Soul in Rabbinic Literature of the Talmudic Period*. Edward Goldstone, 1947.

Hoberman, J. *Bridge of Light: Yiddish Film Between Two Worlds*. Temple University Press, 1995.

Hoffman, Edward. *The Way of Splendor: Jewish Mysticism and Modern Psychology*. Shambhala, 1981.

Hoffman, Wayne. "A 'Fiddler' in Tokyo." *Tablet*. January 8, 2018, tabletmag.com/scroll/252671/a-fiddler-in-tokyo

Horowitz, Elliott. "Speaking to the Dead: Cemetery Prayer in Medieval and Early Modern Jewry." *The Journal of Jewish Thought and Philosophy* 8, (1999): 303-17.

Isherwood, Charles, "A Dybbuk, or Between Two Worlds." *Variety*, November 29th, 1997.

Joachim, Neugroschel, ed. and trans. *The Dybbuk and the Yiddish Imagination: A Haunted Reader*. Syracuse University Press, 2000.

Naveh, Joseph and Shaked, Shaul. *Amulets and Magic Bowls: Aramaic Incantations of Late Antiquity*. Magnes Press, 1987.

Litvak, Olga. *The Romantic Movement in Judaism*. Rutgers University Press, 2012.

Liptzin, Sol. *The Flowering of Yiddish Literature*. Thomas Yoseloff, 1963.

———. *A History of Yiddish Literature*. Jonathan David Publishers, 1985.

Legutko, Agnieszka. "Possessed by the Other: Dybbuk Possession and Modern Jewish Identity in Twentieth-Century Jewish Literature and Beyond." Doctoral Dissertation, Columbia University, 2012.

Madison, Charles. *Yiddish Literature: Its Scope and Major Writers from Mendele and Sholem Aleichem to Isaac Bashevis Singer*. Schocken Books, 1971

Malkiel, David. "Between Worldliness and Traditionalism: Eighteenth-Century Jews Debate Intercessory Prayer." *Jewish Studies, an Internet Journal* 2, (2003): 169-98

Nigel, Gedalyah. *Magic, Mysticism and Hasidism: The Supernatural in Jewish Thought*. Translated by Edward Levin. Jason Aronson, 1994.

Patai, Raphael. *Gates to the Old City*. Jason Aronson Publishers, 1998.

Paull, Simcha Steven [Simcha Raphael]. "Judaism's Contribution to the Psychology of Death and Dying." PhD diss., California Institute of Integral Studies, 1986.

Peñasola, Fernando. *The Dybbuk: Text, Subtext, and Context*. Tsiterboym Books, 2012.

Peretz, I.L. *The I.L. Peretz Reader*. Edited by Ruth R. Wisse. Schocken Books, 1990.

Pine, Dan, "Feminist Twist on Yiddish Classic in Operatic Dybbuk" *Jewish News of Northern California*. September 16th, 2016.

Pollack, Herman, *Jewish Folkways in Germanic Lands (1648-1806) - Studies in Aspects of Daily Life*. MIT Press, 1971.

Raphael, Simcha Paull. *Jewish Views of the Afterlife*. 3rd ed. Rowman & Littlefield, 2019.

Raphael, Simcha Paull, Dayle A. Friedman, and David Levin, eds. *Jewish End-of-Life Care in a Virtual Age: Our Traditions Reimagined*. Albion-Andalus Books, 2021.

Safran, Gabriella. "Dancing with Death and Salvaging Jewish Culture in Austria and The Dybbuk" *Slavic Review* 5, no. 4 (2000): 761-81.

————— . *Wandering Soul: The Dybbuk's Creator, S. An-sky.* Harvard University Press, 2010.

Safran, Gabriella and Zipperstein, Steven J., eds. *The Worlds of S. An-sky: A Russian Jewish Intellectual at the Turn of the Century.* Stanford University Press, 2006.

Schachter-Shalomi, Zalman. "Life in the Hereafter: A Tour of What's to Come." In *The Jewish Almanac*, edited by Richard Siegel and Carl Rheins, 594–96. Bantam Books, 1980.

Scholem, Gershom, *Sabbatai Ṣevi: The Mystical Messiah, 1626–1676,* Translated by Zvi Werblowsky. Princeton University Press, 2016.

Sered, Susan Starr. "Rachel's Tomb: The Development of a Cult" *Jewish Studies Quarterly* 2, No. 2 (1995): 103-148.

Shevitz, Daniel R. "Rituals for Jewish Exorcism." *The Jewish Almanac.* Edited by Richard Siegel and Carl Rheins. Bantam Books, 1980.

Shyovitz, David I. "You Have Saved Me From the Judgment of Gehenna: The Origins of the Kaddish in Medieval Ashkenaz." *AJS Review* 39:1 (April 2015): 49–73.

Singer, Isaac Bashevis. *A Little Boy in Search of God or Mysticism in a Personal Light.* Doubleday, 1976

————. *Shadows on the Hudson.* Translated by Joseph Sherman. Farrar, Straus and Giroux, 1998.

————. *The Family Moskat.* Translated by A.H. Gross. Farrar, Straus and Giroux, 1950.

————. *The Magician of Lublin.* Translated by Elaine Gottlieb and Joseph Singer. Farrar, Straus and Giroux, 1960.

————. *Satan in Goray.* Translated by A.H. Gross. Farrar, Straus and Giroux, 1955.

————. "Sabbath in Gehenna" in *The Death of Methuselah and Other Stories.* Faffar, Straus and Giroux,1988.

Starr, Zachary Alan. *Toward A History of Jewish Thought: The Soul, Resurrection, and the Afterlife*. Wipf and Stock, 2022.

Taylor, Brian, "Taking Soul Birds Seriously: A Post-Secular Animist Perspective on Extra-Ordinary Communications" *Paranthropology: Anthropological Approaches to the Paranormal* 6, No. 2 (July 2015).

Tolstoy, Leo. *Death of Ivan Illych*. Translated by Lynn Solotaroff. Bantam Books, 1981.

Trachtenberg, Joshua. *Jewish Magic and Superstition: A Study in Folk Religion*. Atheneum, 1974.

Verney, Thomas and Kelly, John. *The Secret Life of the Unborn Child: How You Can Prepare Your Unborn Baby for a Happy, Healthy Life*. Bantam Dell Publishing, 1981.

Waxman, Meyer. *A History of Jewish Literature*. Thomas Yoseloff Ltd., 1960.

Weiss, Abner. *Death and Bereavement: A Halakhic Guide*. Ktav Publishing House Inc., 1991.

Weissler ,Chava, "The Traditional Piety of Ashkenazic Women" in *Jewish Spirituality, Vol. 2: From the Sixteenth Century Revival to the Present*. Edited by Arthur Green. Crossroad Publishing, 1987.

Wiener, Leo. *History of Yiddish Literature in the Nineteenth Century*, 2nd Edition. Herman Press, 1972.

Winkler, Gershon. *Dybbuk*. Judaica, Press. 1982.

Wisse, Ruth R., "Peretz, Yitskhok Leybush." *YIVO Encyclopedia of Jews in Eastern Europe*. yivoencyclopedia.org/article.aspx/Peretz_Yitskhok_Leybush

Wieseltier, Leon. *Kaddish*. Alfred A. Knopf, 1998.

Yivrov, Tzvi. *L'illui Neshamah*. n.p. 2008.

The Da'at Institute
Melrose Park, PA, 19027
drsimcha@daatinstitute.net
daatinstitute.net

The DA'AT INSTITUTE is dedicated to providing death awareness education and professional development training. Working in consultation with synagogues, churches, hospice programs and other types of community organizations, the DA'AT INSTITUTE offers:

1. *Educational Programs* on death, dying, bereavement, and the spirituality of end-of-life issues and concerns.

2. *Professional Development Training* to clergy, health care and mental health professionals and educators working with the dying and bereaved.

3. *Bereavement and Hospice Counseling Services* to individuals and families through counseling, professional referral and bereavement support groups.

4. *Rituals of Transition* for dying, burial, bereavement, unveiling and memorialization, helping families create meaningful rituals of passage.

5. *Printed and Audio-Visual Resources* on the various facets of dealing with grief and loss, and on the spirituality of death and afterlife.

Originally from Montreal, Canada, Simcha Paull Raphael, Ph.D. is Founding Director of the DA'AT Institute for Death Awareness, Advocacy and Training. He received a Master of Arts in History and Philosophy of Religion from Concordia University, a doctorate in Psychology from the California Institute of Integral Studies, and was ordained as a Rabbinic Chaplain by Reb Zalman Schachter-Shalomi. He has served as Adjunct Professor at LaSalle University, Temple University and in the Aleph Ordination Program. Currently, he works as a psychotherapist and spiritual director in the Philadelphia area, and is on Faculty of the Art of Dying Institute of the School of American Thanatology. He has published seven books on death and Judaism, including the groundbreaking *Jewish Views of the Afterlife* and a collection of poetry, *Echoes from the Ashes: Holocaust Poems of Life, Death and Re-Birth*. Reb Simcha and his wife, Rabbi Geela Rayzel Raphael live in the Philadelphia area with their son Yigdal and daughter Hallel.

www.ingramcontent.com/pod-product-compliance
Lightning Source LLC
Chambersburg PA
CBHW021102130626
46554CB00002B/487